T0126876

BASEBALL EPIC

Also from Coffee House Press

How to Be Perfect: An Illustrated Guide
by Ron Padgett, with pictures by Jason Novak

BASEBALL EPIC

FAMOUS AND FORGOTTEN LIVES OF THE DEAD BALL ERA

WORDS AND
PICTURES BY
JASON NOVAK

COFFEE HOUSE PRESS

MINNEAPOLIS

2019

Cover design by Kyle G. Hunter
Author photograph © Rachel Sher

Coffee House Press books are available to the trade through our primary distributor, Consortium Book Sales & Distribution, cbsd.com or (800) 283-3572. For personal orders, catalogs, or other information, write to info@coffeehousepress.org.

Coffee House Press is a nonprofit literary publishing house. Support from private foundations, corporate giving programs, government programs, and generous individuals helps make the publication of our books possible. We gratefully acknowledge their support in detail in the back of this book.

LIBRARY OF CONGRESS CATALOGING-IN-PUBLICATION DATA

Names: Novak, Jason, 1979– author.
Title: Baseball epic : famous and forgotten lives of the dead ball era / Jason Novak.
Description: Minneapolis : Coffee House Press, 2019.
Identifiers: LCCN 2018027630 | ISBN 9781566895422 (paper over board)
Subjects: LCSH: Baseball players—United States—Biography. |
Baseball—United States—History—20th century.
Classification: LCC GV865.A1 N68 2019 | DDC 796.357092/2 [B] —dc23
LC record available at https://lccn.loc.gov/2018027630

PRINTED IN CANADA

26 25 24 23 22 21 20 19 1 2 3 4 5 6 7 8

BASEBALL EPIC

EVERY PERSON IN THIS BOOK PLAYED PROFESSIONAL BASEBALL BETWEEN 1900 AND 1920, IN WHAT'S KNOWN AS THE DEAD BALL ERA. THE SYMBOLIC BEGINNING OF THE ERA WAS THE FIRST WORLD SERIES IN 1903, AND ITS SYMBOLIC END WAS THE INFAMOUS 1919 WORLD SERIES, IN WHICH SEVERAL PLAYERS FOR THE CHICAGO WHITE SOX WERE ACCUSED OF ACCEPTING BRIBES TO THROW GAMES.

AD BRENNAN, WHOSE PLAYING CAREER WAS OVERSHADOWED BY AN INCIDENT IN WHICH HE PUNCHED GIANTS MANAGER JOHN MCGRAW OFF HIS FEET, WAS PLAGUED THROUGHOUT HIS LIFE WITH THROAT AILMENTS FOR OVERUSING SPITBALLS.

ALBERT "CHIEF" BENDER, WHO WAS CHIPPEWA, ENDURED RELENTLESS TAUNTS, INSULTS, AND WAR WHOOPS FROM THE BLEACHERS, BUT WOULD CIRCLE THE STADIUM FOLLOWING A VICTORY AND YELL, "FOREIGNERS! FOREIGNERS!"

ARMANDO MARSANS, A CUBAN WHO FELL INTO THE GRAY AREA OF SEGREGATED AMERICA, PLAYED IN BOTH THE MAJOR AND NEGRO LEAGUES. WITH THE BENEFIT OF A TOBACCO FORTUNE BACK IN HAVANA, MARSANS WAS WILLING TO RISK BREAKING HIS CONTRACT, A MOVE THAT ENDED HIS CAREER IN THE MAJORS.

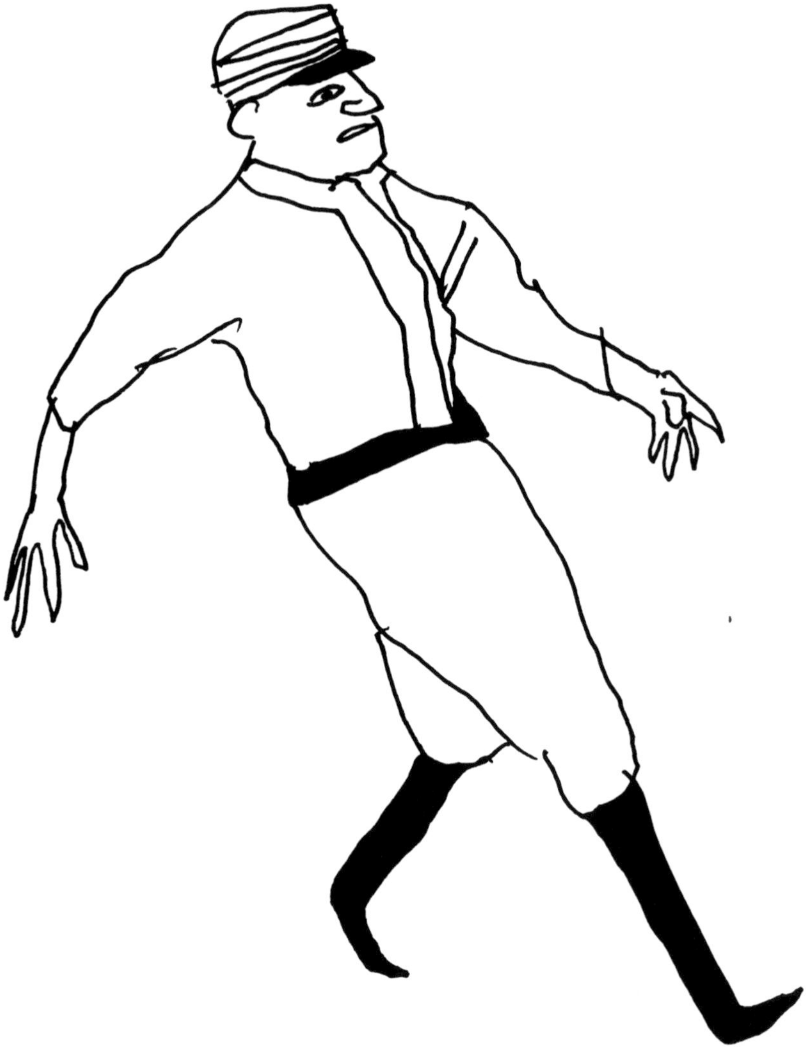

BENNY KAUFF, KNOWN FOR HIS FASHIONABLE CLOTHING BOTH ON AND OFF THE FIELD, WAS IMPLICATED IN THE RIGGING OF THE 1919 WORLD SERIES AND BANNED FROM PLAYING. HE SPENT HIS FINAL YEARS AS A CLOTHING SALESMAN,

BILL BERNHARD, WHO
MANAGED MINOR LEAGUE
TEAMS IN AN ERA WHEN
EVEN THE MAJORS PAID
POORLY, WAS ONCE ASKED
HOW MUCH A PLAYER SHOULD
MAKE. "ANYTHING HE CAN GET,"
WAS THE REPLY.

Bill Cunningham died
of a heart attack
after catching a
twenty-eight-pound
salmon in the
Sacramento River.

BILL HOBBS, WHO WAS ONCE
KNOCKED UNCONSCIOUS FOR
TWENTY HOURS BY A PITCH
TO THE HEAD, LATER
ACCIDENTALLY FATALLY
SHOT HIMSELF WHILE
HUNTING RABBITS.

BILL MONROE WAS KNOWN IN THE NEGRO LEAGUES FOR PLAYING WITH ACROBATIC FLAIR, AND FOR HIS SHARP WIT. WHEN ASKED HIS OCCUPATION BY THE CENSUS BUREAU, MONROE REPLIED, "CHAMPION BASEBALL PLAYER."

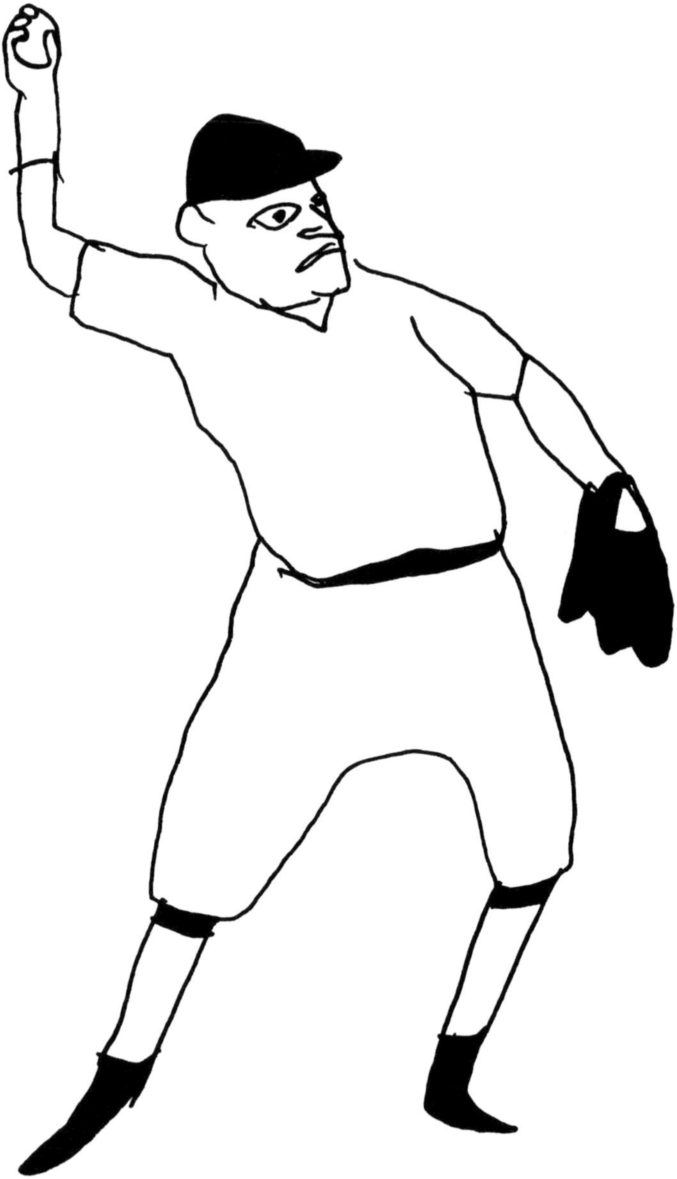

BIRDIE CREE ONCE
FOUND A BALL HE'D HIT
OUT OF THE PARK IN A
SALOON ACROSS THE STREET.

BLUE WASHINGTON LEFT
PITCHING IN THE NEGRO LEAGUES
FOR HOLLYWOOD, APPEARING
IN OVER SEVENTY FILMS
ALONGSIDE BUSTER KEATON,
JACKIE GLEASON, AND
JOHN WAYNE.

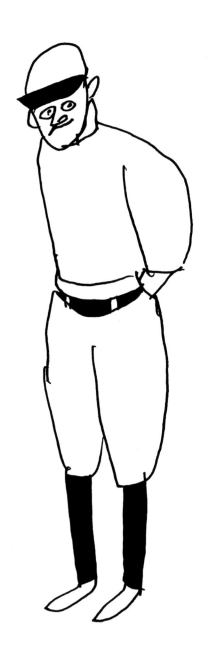

BOSS SCHMIDT, WHO DIVIDED HIS TIME WITH PROFESSIONAL BOXING, ONCE BROKE NOTORIOUSLY COMBATIVE PLAYER TY COBB'S NOSE IN A FIGHT.

BRANCH RICKEY, AS MANAGER OF HIS COLLEGE TEAM, PROMISED THE TEAM'S SOLE BLACK PLAYER THAT HE'D DO WHATEVER HE COULD TO FIGHT SEGREGATION IN BASEBALL. NEARLY FIFTY YEARS LATER, AS PRESIDENT OF THE DODGERS, RICKEY SIGNED JACKIE ROBINSON, ENDING SEGREGATION IN THE MAJORS.

BUCK HERZOG SHREWDLY
NEGOTIATED HIGH CONTRACTS
AS A PLAYER, BUT SPENT
HIS FINAL YEARS BROKE
IN A RESIDENCE HOTEL.

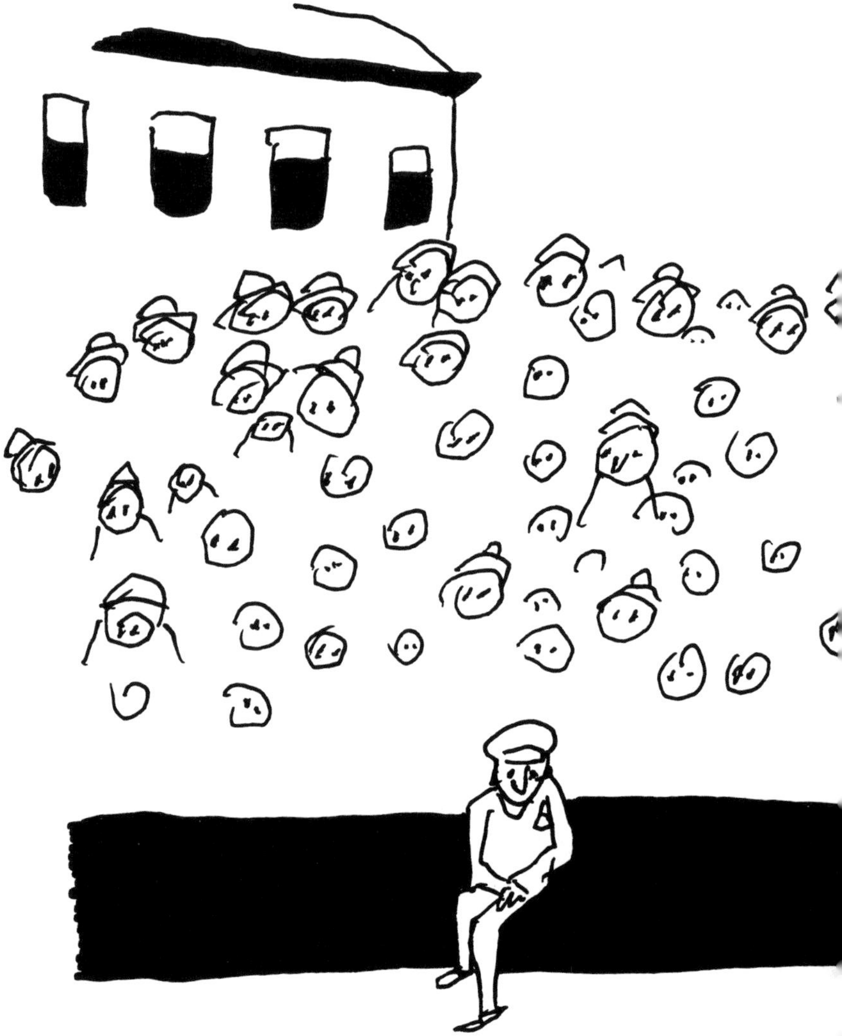

BAKER BOWL IN PHILADELPHIA WAS ORIGINALLY BUILT ENTIRELY OUT OF WOOD.

IT WAS DURING A GAME THAT A
FIGHT ON THE STREET OUTSIDE THE PARK
CREATED A RUSH ON THE BLEACHERS,
CAUSING THEM TO COLLAPSE AND KILL
TWELVE PEOPLE.

CAL VASBINDER'S PLAYING CAREER ENDED WHEN HIS LEGS WERE HORRIBLY MANGLED IN A MINING ACCIDENT.

CANDY LACHANCE ONCE
GOT INTO A WRESTLING
MATCH WITH A RIVAL PLAYER
BEFORE A GAME, LOSING
BOTH THE MATCH AND
THE GAME.

CHARLIE ARMBRUSTER
MADE IT TO THE AGE OF
EIGHTY-FOUR BEFORE HE
ACCIDENTALLY SHOT
HIMSELF WHILE CLEANING
HIS GUN.

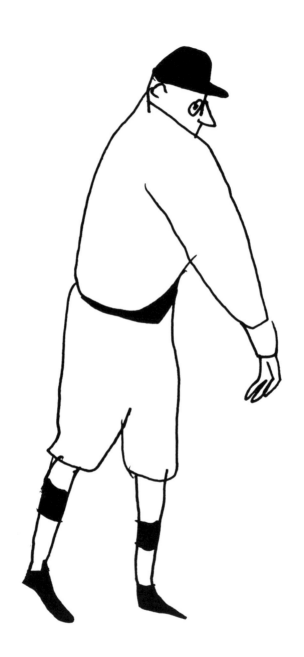

CHARLIE FAUST WAS TOLD
BY A FORTUNE-TELLER THAT
PITCHING FOR THE GIANTS WOULD
WIN THEM THE PENNANT. SUPER-
STITIOUS GIANTS MANAGER JOHN
MCGRAW AGREED TO SIGN FAUST
AS PREGAME ENTERTAINMENT.
THE GIANTS WON THE PENNANT
AND FAUST REMAINED ON THE
TEAM UNTIL HIS MADNESS BECAME
UNMANAGEABLE. FOUND WANDERING
IN DELIRIUM AROUND PORTLAND,
OREGON, FAUST WAS SENT TO
AN ASYLUM, WHERE HE DIED,

CHARLIE GRANT WAS
WORKING AS A HOTEL
PORTER WHEN VACATIONING
GIANTS MANAGER JOHN
MCGRAW DISCOVERED
HIM AND TRIED TO
SIGN HIM AS A
"CHEROKEE INDIAN."
HIS RECEPTION AMONG
FRIENDS IN THE PRE-
SEASON GAVE HIM AWAY
AS A BLACK PLAYER.
GRANT WAS LATER
KILLED BY AN ERRANT
VEHICLE WHILE SITTING
ON A SIDEWALK IN
CINCINNATI.

CHICK STAHL DRANK A LETHAL DOSE OF CARBOLIC ACID. A YEAR LATER, HIS WIDOW WAS FOUND DEAD IN THE DOORWAY OF A TENEMENT UNDER MYSTERIOUS CIRCUMSTANCES.

CHRISTY MATHEWSON,
A SUPERSTAR OF HIS TIME
AND AUTHOR OF A LONG-
FORGOTTEN CHILDREN'S BOOK,
"SECOND BASE SLOAN,"
CONTRACTED A FATAL
CASE OF TUBERCULOSIS
AFTER EXPOSURE TO
CHEMICAL GAS IN
WORLD WAR ONE.

COUNTRY BROWN, A PRANKSTER
IN THE NEGRO LEAGUES KNOWN
TO SOMETIMES BAT ON HIS
KNEES, WAS KILLED IN A FIGHT
WITH HIS BROTHER-IN-LAW
ON CHRISTMAS DAY.

CRISTÓBAL TORRIENTE, AN
AFRO-CUBAN WHO PLAYED IN THE
NEGRO LEAGUES, AND WHO ONCE
SPUN THE HAND ON A CLOCK
TOWER WITH A HOME RUN,
DRANK HIMSELF TO DEATH
ON HIS OWN MOONSHINE.

CY WILLIAMS, WHO STUDIED ARCHITECTURE AT NOTRE DAME, RETIRED TO WISCONSIN AFTER BASEBALL, WHERE HE GAINED A REPUTATION FOR DESIGNING AND CONSTRUCTING UNUSUAL BUILDINGS.

DAVE BROWN, TOP PITCHER IN THE NEGRO LEAGUES, WAS THE SUBJECT OF AN FBI MANHUNT AFTER KILLING A MAN IN A BAR FIGHT. HE WAS NEVER FOUND.

DICK LUNDY,
A NEGRO LEAGUER,
WENT BLIND AND
ENDED HIS DAYS
SHINING SHOES.

DICK REDDING, KNOWN IN
THE NEGRO LEAGUES AS
"CANNONBALL" FOR HIS
PITCHING ARM, WAS DUBBED
"GRENADE" AFTER HIS SERVICE
IN WORLD WAR ONE.
REDDING SPENT HIS FINAL
DECADE IN AN ASYLUM.

DOBIE MOORE, A RISING STAR IN THE NEGRO LEAGUES, WAS TUSSLING WITH A WOMAN IN HER APARTMENT WHEN SHE SHOT HIM IN THE LEG. MOORE LEAPT FROM THE BALCONY, FURTHER SHATTERING HIS ALREADY INJURED LEG, AND PERMANENTLY ENDING HIS BASEBALL CAREER.

DOC POWERS, SO NAMED
FOR GRADUATING FROM MEDICAL
SCHOOL, WAS INJURED IN THE
FIRST GAME EVER PLAYED AT
SHIBE PARK IN PHILADELPHIA.
THE INJURY REVEALED A FATAL
INTESTINAL ILLNESS THAT
CLAIMED HIM AFTER FAILED
SURGERIES.

DODE PASKERT ONCE CARRIED FIVE CHILDREN OUT OF A BURNING APARTMENT BUILDING IN CLEVELAND, SEVEN YEARS AFTER ACCIDENTALLY FATALLY HITTING A CHILD WITH HIS CAR IN A CROWDED CLEVELAND STREET.

ED CERMAK WAS
RENDERED MUTE AFTER
GETTING HIT IN THE
THROAT BY A BASEBALL
WHILE UMPIRING.
HE DIED LATER THAT
YEAR FROM TUBERCULOSIS.

ED DELAHANTY WAS
DRUNK AND BRANDISHING
A RAZOR WHEN KICKED OFF
A TRAIN TO NEW YORK.
CROSSING THE INTERNATIONAL
RAILWAY BRIDGE ON FOOT,
HE FELL TO HIS DEATH
IN NIAGARA FALLS.

ED DOHENY AT THE APEX
OF HIS CAREER HAD A SLOW
AND INCREASINGLY VIOLENT
NERVOUS BREAKDOWN THAT
LED TO INSTITUTIONALIZATION
FOR THE FINAL DOZEN
YEARS OF HIS LIFE,

HILLTOP PARK IN MANHATTAN WAS BUILT ON GROUND THAT WAS OVERRUN WITH HESSIAN MERCENARIES WHEN BRITISH FORCES TOOK FORT WASHINGTON DURING THE REVOLUTIONARY WAR.

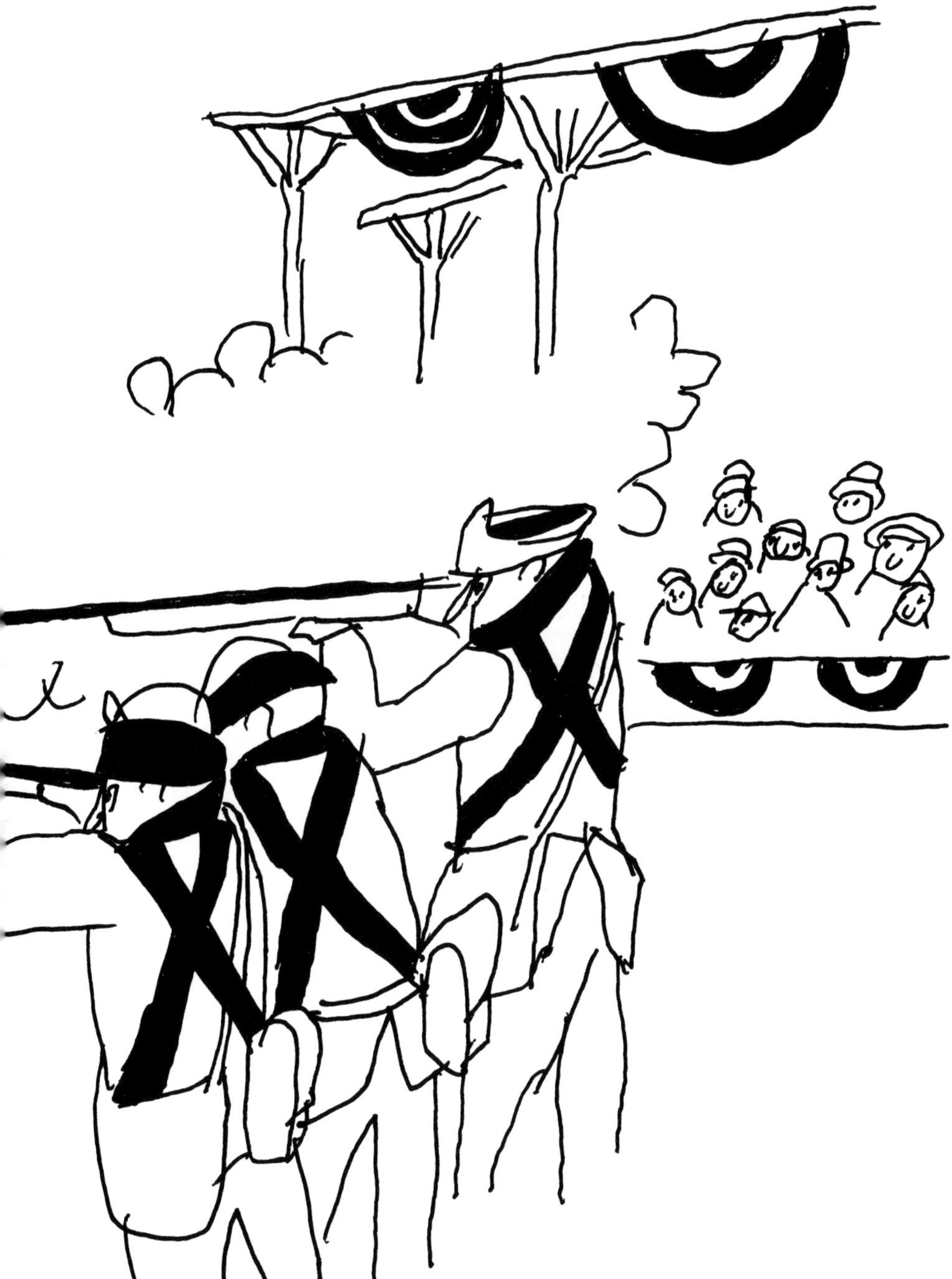

EDDIE CICOTTE, BANNED FROM
BASEBALL FOR HIS ROLE IN THE
RIGGING OF THE 1919 WORLD
SERIES, ENDED HIS DAYS AS A
STRAWBERRY FARMER IN MICHIGAN.
CONTRITE TO THE END, HE
WOULD PATIENTLY ANSWER MAIL
FROM PEOPLE CURIOUS ABOUT
THE SCANDAL.

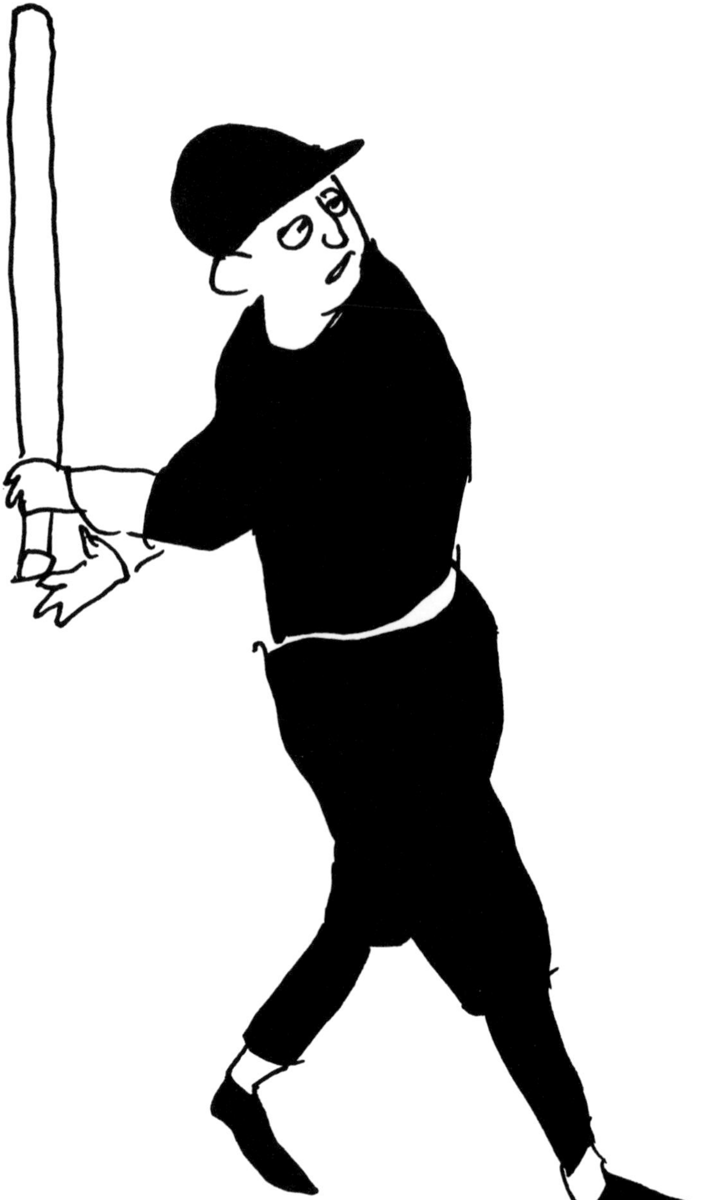

EDDIE GRANT, A BASKETBALL
STAR AT HARVARD, WAS LEADING
HIS BATTALION THROUGH THE
ARGONNE FOREST IN WORLD
WAR ONE WHEN HE WAS HIT
BY A MORTAR SHELL AND
KILLED INSTANTLY,

ELI CATES WAS FORCED
OUT OF BASEBALL WHEN
HIS ARM WAS SMASHED
IN A CORN THRESHER.

FRANK BLATTNER, AN IOWA NATIVE, PLAYED WITH THE ALL-NATIONS TEAM, BILLING HIMSELF AS A HAWAIIAN NAMED "BLUKOI."

FRANK CHANCE, A BELLIGERENT PLAYER KNOWN TO THROW BEER BOTTLES AT HECKLERS DURING GAMES, WAS BEANED SO MANY TIMES AT BAT THAT HE EVENTUALLY DIED FROM HEAD INJURIES,

FRANK CORRIDON, WHO
PLAYED CONCERT VIOLIN IN
THE OFF-SEASON, IS CREDITED
WITH DEVELOPING THE SPITBALL
AFTER ACCIDENTALLY GETTING
THE BALL WET DURING PRACTICE,
THOUGH HE RARELY USED
IT DURING GAMES. HE WOULD
LATER NARROWLY LOSE A
BID FOR A SEAT IN THE
RHODE ISLAND LEGISLATURE,

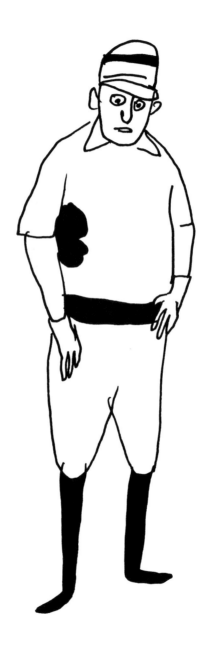

FRED BROWN WOULD
EVENTUALLY BECOME THE
GOVERNOR OF NEW HAMPSHIRE.
A STROKE LEFT HIM
INCAPACITATED FOR
THE LAST FIFTEEN YEARS
OF HIS LIFE.

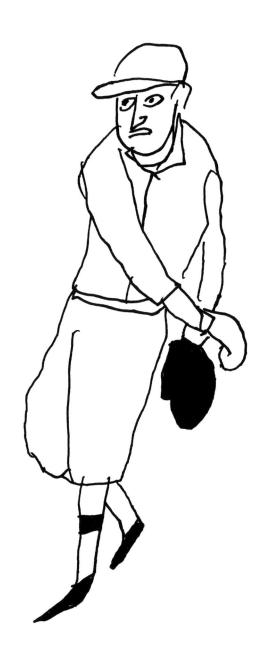

FRED LUDERUS ONCE
THWARTED A PITCHER
FAMOUS FOR SPITBALLS
BY COATING THE BALL
IN HOT LINIMENT.
THE PITCHER WAS
BENCHED WITH A SWOLLEN
TONGUE. LUDERUS
WOULD GO ON TO START
A TOY COMPANY THAT
MADE ANIMALS OUT
OF YARN.

GEORGE BAUMGARDNER, A SEMILITERATE FARM BOY FROM WEST VIRGINIA, WAS PAID BY HIS TEAM IN DOLLAR BILLS SO THAT IT WOULD LOOK LIKE MORE MONEY. AFTER LEAVING BASEBALL TO SERVE DURING WORLD WAR ONE, BAUMGARDNER SPENT THE REMAINING FIFTY YEARS OF HIS LIFE AS AN UNEMPLOYED RECLUSE IN HIS HOME TOWN.

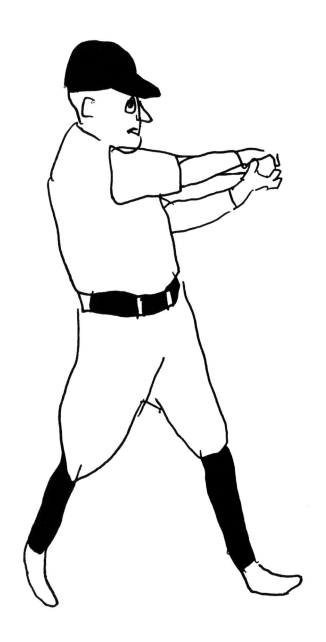

GEORGE DAVIS, CHASED
FOR YEARS BY RUMORS
OF AFFAIRS AND INFIDELITIES,
DIED IN AN INSTITUTION
OF SYPHILITIC DEMENTIA,

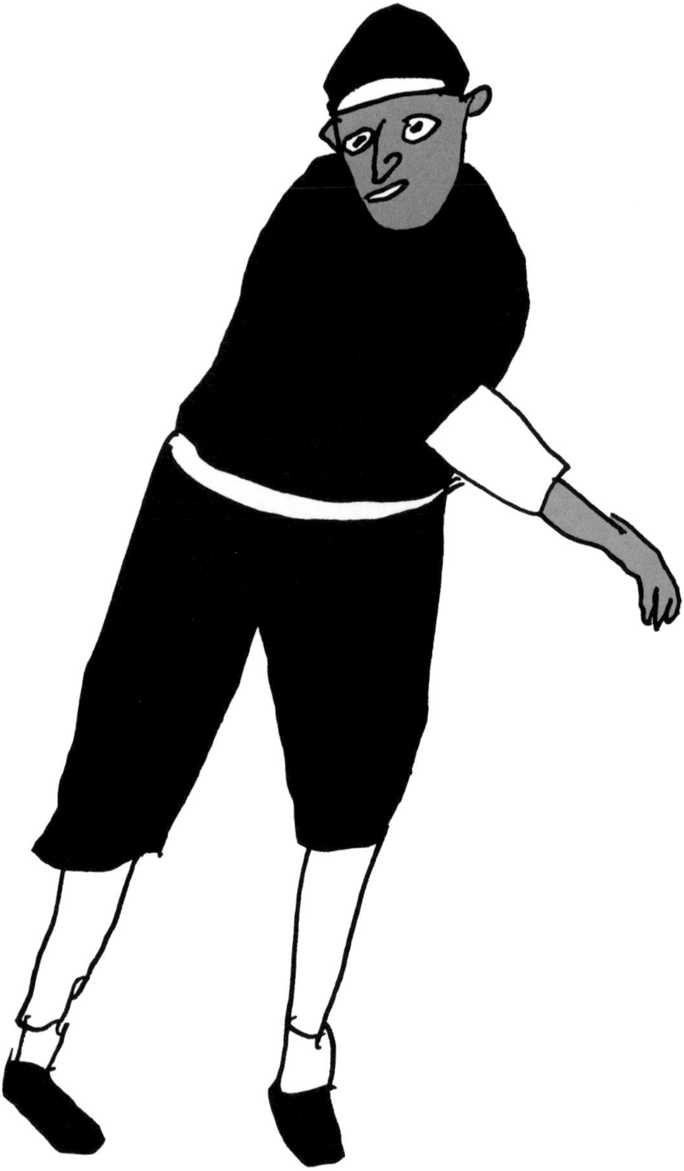

GEORGE "CHIEF" JOHNSON, A WINNEBAGO, RAN A MEDICINE SHOW WHILE BARNSTORMING WITH INDEPENDENT TEAMS AROUND THE MIDWEST. IT WAS DURING A MEDICINE SHOW IN IOWA THAT HE WAS SHOT DEAD OVER A GAME OF DICE.

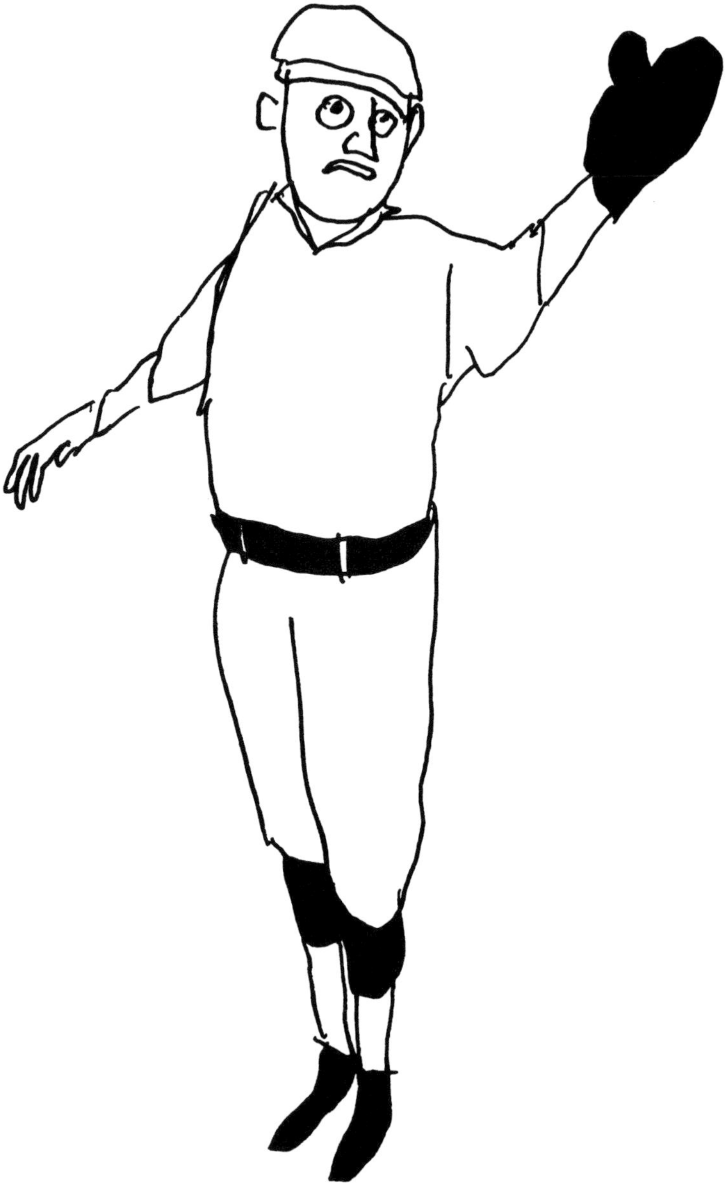

GERMANY SCHAEFER WOULD
SOMETIMES TAKE THE FIELD
WEARING RAIN GEAR IN AN
ATTEMPT TO HAVE THE GAME
DECLARED A RAINOUT.
LONG STRICKEN WITH
TUBERCULOSIS, SCHAEFER
COUGHED HIMSELF TO DEATH
ON A TRAIN IN UPSTATE
NEW YORK.

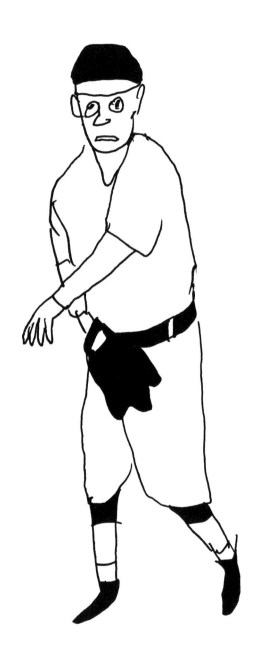

HAL CHASE, IMPLICATED IN THE RIGGING OF THE 1919 WORLD SERIES, LEFT THE MAJOR LEAGUES TO COURT SCANDAL IN THE MINORS, AND FINALLY DRANK A SERIES OF BUSINESSES INTO THE GROUND. "MY LIFE," HE SAID, "HAS BEEN ONE GREAT BIG MISTAKE AFTER ANOTHER."

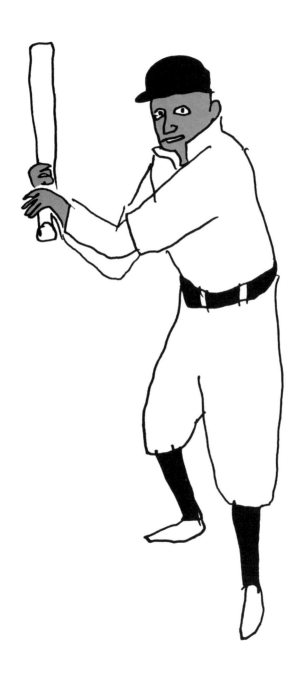

HOME RUN JOHNSON, WHO PLAYED FOR NEGRO TEAMS WELL INTO HIS FIFTIES, ONCE SAID OF STRIKING OUT, "WHEN I DID, I SURPRISED MYSELF."

HONUS WAGNER, A TITAN OF EARLY BASEBALL, RAN FOR SHERIFF IN HIS HOME TOWN AND LOST BY A LANDSLIDE.

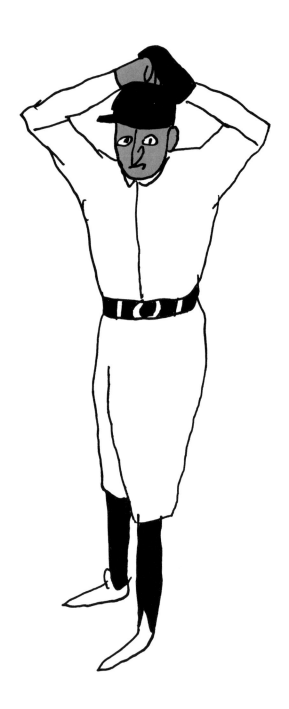

IGNACIO ROJAS COYLY DECLARED ON HIS WORLD WAR ONE DRAFT CARD THAT HE WAS A "FARMER" EMPLOYED BY THE OWNER OF A TEAM IN THE PACIFIC COAST LEAGUE.

JACK CALVO, SON OF A CUBAN SUGAR MAGNATE, BRIEFLY PLAYED TWO STINTS IN THE MAJORS BUT WAS SNUBBED BY HIS WORKING-CLASS TEAMMATES. HE OPTED TO PLAY IN THE MINOR LEAGUES FOR THE REST OF HIS CAREER, SPENDING WINTERS AS A POLICE LIEUTENANT IN CUBA. CALVO LIVED LONG ENOUGH TO WEATHER THE CUBAN REVOLUTION AND DIED IN MIAMI.

JACK QUINN, A HUNGARIAN BY BIRTH, GOT HIS FIRST CONTRACT AFTER CATCHING A BALL IN THE BLEACHERS AND TOSSING IT STRAIGHT BACK INTO THE CATCHER'S MITT. HE RETIRED FROM THE MAJORS AT AGE FIFTY, A RECORD FOR THE TIME.

JAKE BECKLEY WAS
CONSIDERED HANDSOME
IN SPITE OF A CROSSED
EYE AND AN UNFASH-
IONABLY LARGE
MUSTACHE. HE WAS
KNOWN TO SOMETIMES
WIELD THE WRONG
END OF HIS BAT AT
PLATE.

JAP BARBEAU PLAYED
ALONGSIDE STAR HONOS
WAGNER, WHO ONCE
CELEBRATED A WIN
BY DOFFING THE
DIMINUTIVE BARBEAU'S
HAT TO THE CROWD.

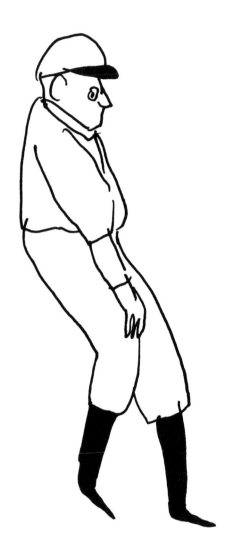

JEAN DUBUC, THOUGH NEVER
FORMALLY CHARGED, QUIETLY
RETREATED INTO THE MINOR
LEAGUES AFTER A FELLOW PLAYER
IMPLICATED HIM IN THE RIGGING
OF THE 1919 WORLD SERIES.
FOLLOWING A STROKE, THE
ONLY WORD THE FRENCH
CANADIAN COULD UTTER
WAS "MERDE".

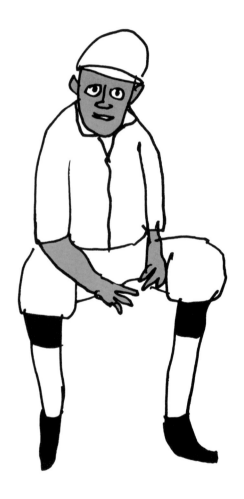

JIM BLUEJACKET, A SHAWNEE, LIVED ON THE ISLAND OF ARUBA FOR FIFTEEN YEARS AS AN EMPLOYEE OF THE STANDARD OIL COMPANY. WHILE THERE, HE ALL BUT SINGLE-HANDEDLY INTRODUCED BASEBALL TO THE LOCALS.

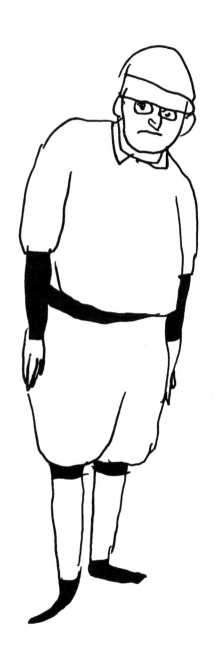

Jim Shaw married a
nurse he met in the
hospital after accidentally
shooting himself while
hunting rabbits. After
baseball, Shaw was an
IRS agent.

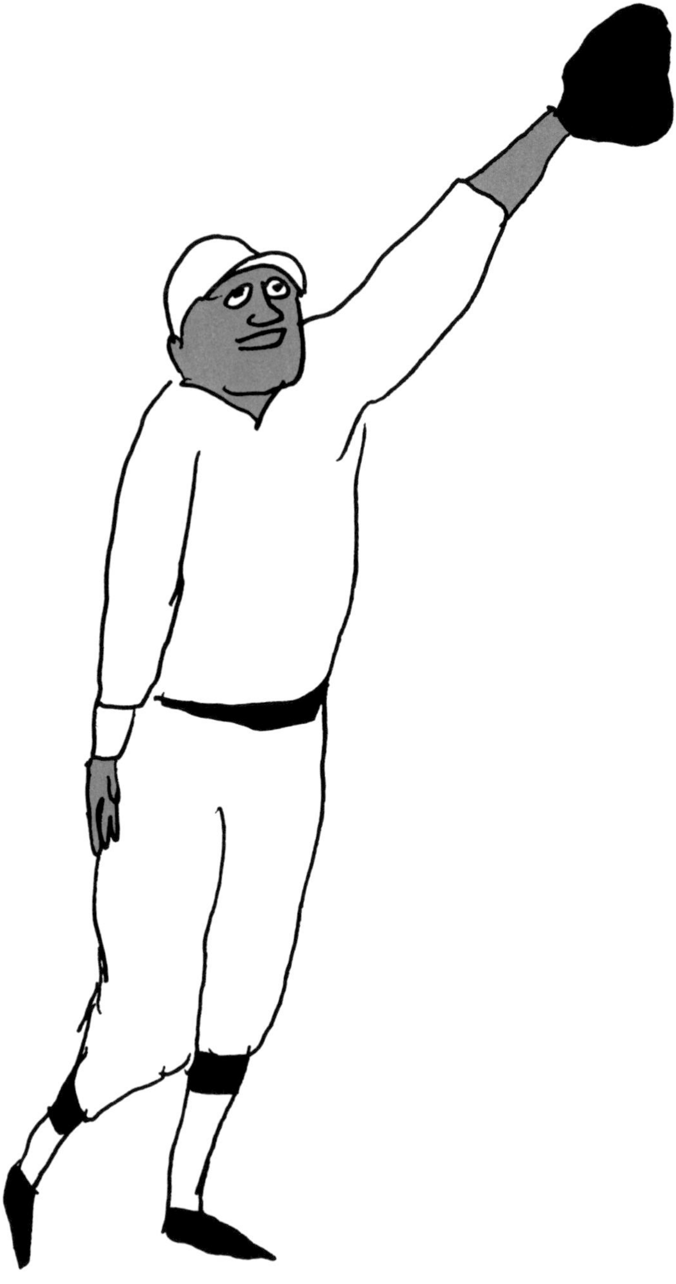

JIM THORPE, SAC AND FOX
INDIAN AND OLYMPIC DECATHLON
GOLD MEDALIST, ONCE PLAYED
A MINOR LEAGUE GAME AGAINST
A YOUNG DWIGHT EISENHOWER.
WHEN IT CAME OUT THAT THORPE
HAD PLAYED SEMIPRO BALL BEFORE
THE OLYMPICS, HIS MEDALS WERE
RESCINDED, ONLY TO BE RESTORED
AFTER HIS DEATH, BUT TOO LATE
TO SALVE HIS HEARTBREAK.

ROBISON FIELD IN ST. LOUIS WAS BUILT ON GROUND THAT HAD ONCE BEEN THE ANCIENT CITY OF CAHOKIA,

WHICH VANISHED MYSTERIOUSLY
NEARLY A THOUSAND YEARS AGO.

JIMMY CLAXTON BROKE
THE COLOR LINE BY
REGISTERING AS AN
"AMERICAN INDIAN"
WITH THE OAKLAND OAKS,
BUT WAS BOOTED WHEN
A SPECTATOR IN THE
BLEACHERS RECOGNIZED
HIM AS A BLACK PLAYER.

JOE GREEN, WHILE PLAYING POSTSEASON WITH A NEGRO TEAM AGAINST THE CHICAGO CUBS, BROKE HIS LEG AT THIRD BASE AND HOPPED ON ONE FOOT TO HOME. HE WOULD RECOVER, BUT YEARS LATER THE INJURY WOULD LEAD TO THE AMPUTATION THAT KILLED HIM.

JOE ROGAN, LIKE MANY OF
HIS COHORTS IN THE NEGRO
LEAGUES, GOT HIS START PLAYING
REGIMENTAL BASEBALL FOR THE
ARMY WHILE STATIONED IN
THE PHILIPPINES.

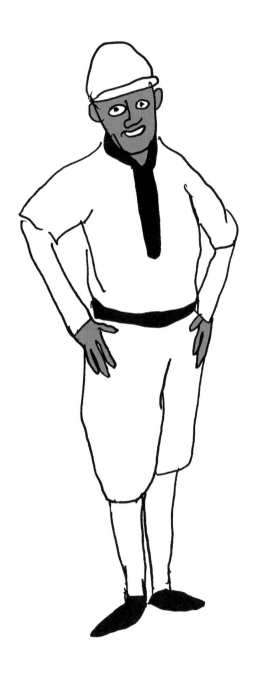

JOHN DONALDSON REJECTED GIANTS MANAGER JOHN McGRAW'S OFFER TO SIGN HIM IF HE POSED AS A CUBAN PLAYER, INSISTING THERE WAS NO SHAME IN BEING BLACK. DONALDSON WENT ON TO BECOME THE FIRST BLACK SCOUT IN THE MAJORS, BUT RESIGNED IN FRUSTRATION WHEN HE WAS BARRED FROM RECRUITING BLACK PLAYERS.

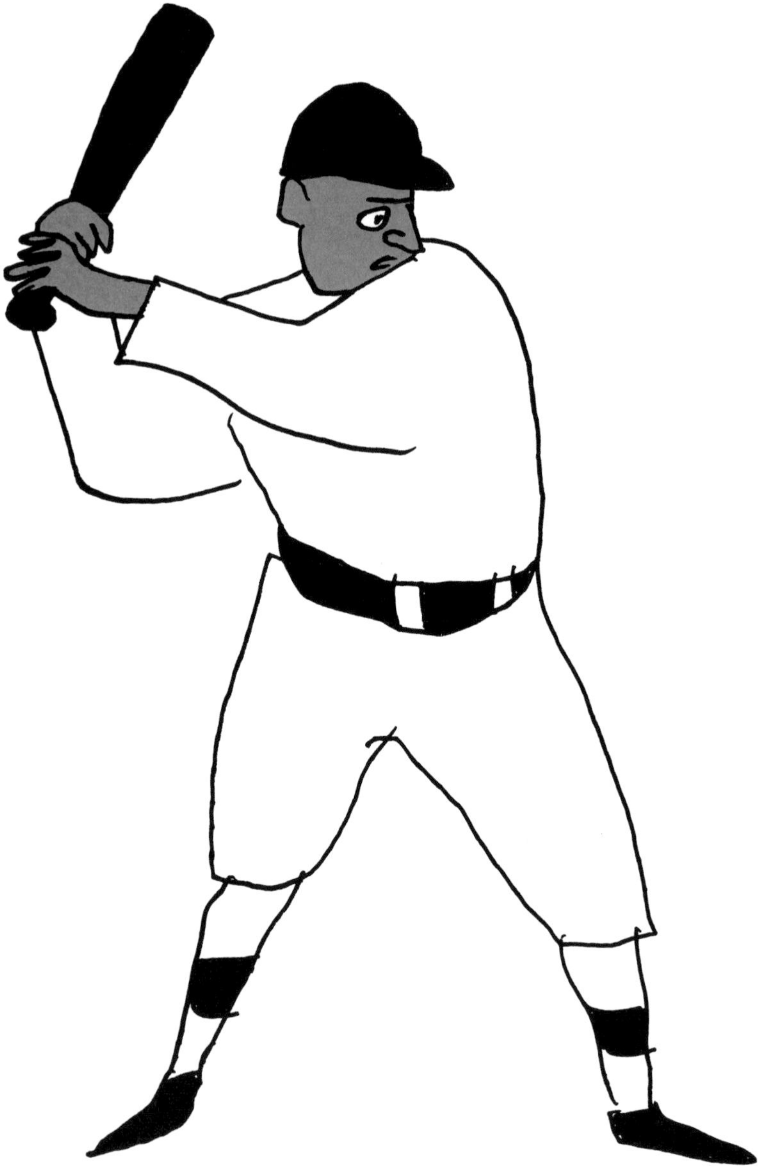

JOHN "CHIEF" MEYERS, A CAHUILLA FROM CALIFORNIA, WENT TO DARTMOUTH WITHOUT COMPLETING HIGH SCHOOL. LATER AS A MAJOR LEAGUER, HE WOULD SPEND HOURS AT ART MUSEUMS DURING GAME RAINOUTS.

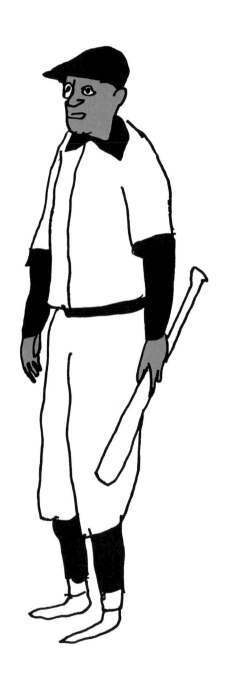

JOSÉ MÉNDEZ, WHO PITCHED
HIS CUBAN TEAM TO LEGENDARY
VICTORIES OVER VISITING TEAMS
FROM THE US MAJOR LEAGUES,
CAUGHT FATAL PNEUMONIA FROM
THE HURRICANE THAT DESTROYED
HIS TEAM'S BALLPARK.

LENA BLACKBURNE'S FORTUNE IN BASEBALL WAS MADE AFTER HIS PLAYING CAREER, WHEN A DEPOSIT OF MUD NEAR HIS HOME PROVED TO BE THE PERFECT RUB FOR SCRUBBING THE SHEEN OFF OF NEW BASEBALLS. BLACKBURNE TURNED IT INTO A PRODUCT THAT CONTINUES TO CORNER THE MARKET.

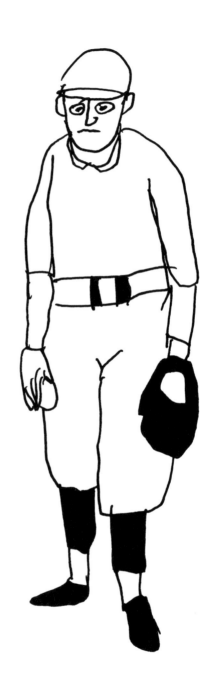

Lizzie Murphy was the first woman to play on a men's team in exhibition games against teams from both the major and Negro leagues. After baseball, she took up clamming in her native Rhode Island.

LOU CASTRO WAS FOND OF NAILING HIS TEAMMATES' SHOES TO THE FLOOR AS A PRANK. FINANCIALLY RUINED DURING THE DEPRESSION, HE DIED IN A PSYCHIATRIC HOSPITAL.

LOUIS SANTOP, A SLUGGER
IN THE NEGRO LEAGUES, ONCE
TOTALED HIS CAR BY KNOCKING
DOWN EVERY TRASH CAN ON
THE OBSTACLE COURSE OF A
DRIVING TEST.

MAE ARBAUGH, THE SOLE WOMAN PLAYING FOR THE ALL-NATIONS TEAM, APPEARED ANONYMOUSLY UNDER THE MONIKER "CARRIE NATION."

MALCOLM MACDONALD WAS
A PATROLMAN IN PHILADELPHIA
PLAYING FOR THE POLICE TEAM
WHEN HE ACCIDENTALLY FATALLY
STRUCK A FRIEND IN THE HEAD
WITH THE BALL. HE LATER RESIGNED
AFTER JUST THREE GAMES IN THE
MAJORS BECAUSE, HE SAID, HE
WASN'T FAST ENOUGH.

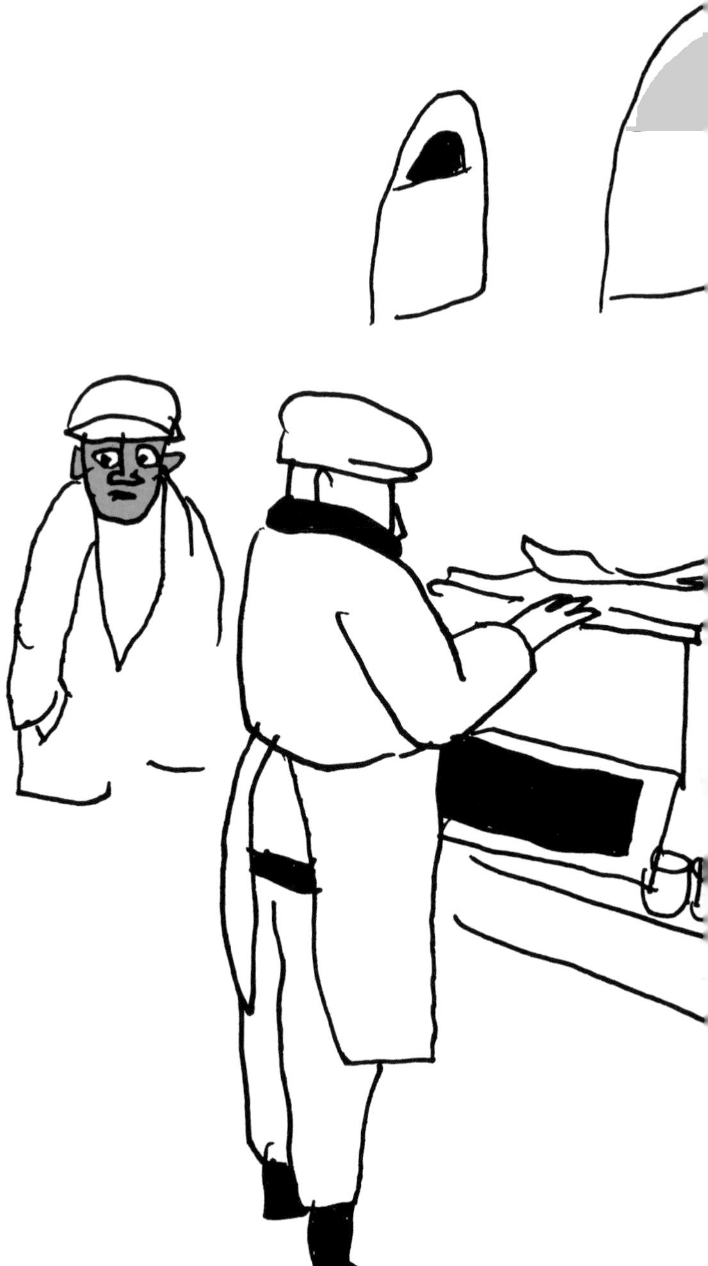

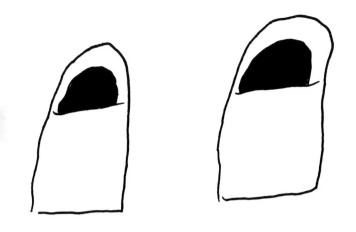

MARTY O'TOOLE WORE HIS ARM OUT PITCHING HIS WAY UP TO THE MAJORS. HE WAS UNABLE TO LIVE UP TO THE HYPE AROUND HIS EXPENSIVE CONTRACT, SO HIS FANS TURNED AGAINST HIM.

AFTER SEVERAL YEARS OF FLOUNDERING, O'TOOLE QUIETLY DISAPPEARED. HIS BODY WAS FOUND BY TRASH COLLECTORS YEARS LATER AT THE BOTTOM OF A FLIGHT OF STAIRS.

MAUD NELSON, STAR PLAYER FOR THE BOSTON BLOOMER GIRLS, AND LATER PLAYER-OWNER OF THE WESTERN BLOOMER GIRLS, REGULARLY BARNSTORMED AGAINST SEMIPRO MEN'S TEAMS.

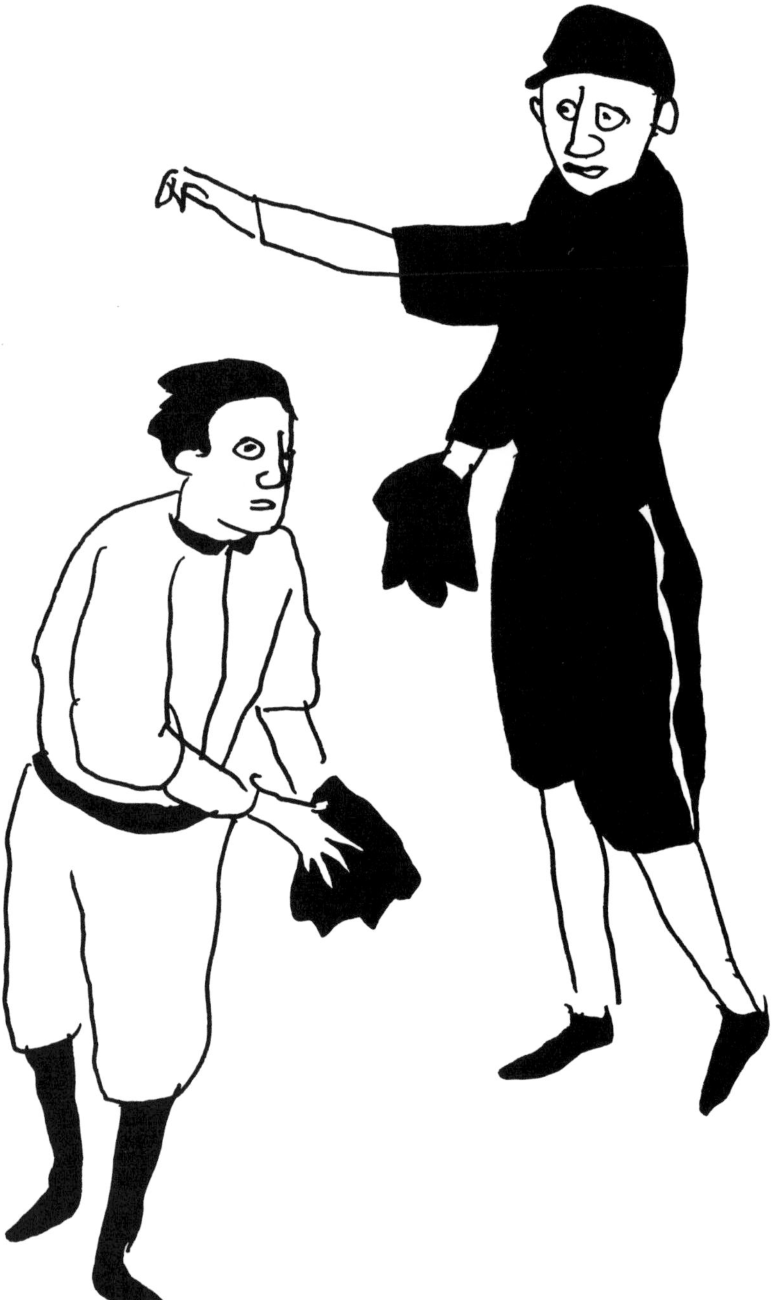

Mike Balenti once played against his uncle, Morrie Rath, though neither knew the other was related.

MIKE DONLIN, HOTHEADED BON VIVANT, SPLIT HIS TIME IN BASEBALL WITH THE VAUDEVILLE STAGE, UNTIL DRINKING ENDED HIS PLAYING CAREER ENTIRELY. MOVIE APPEARANCES ALONGSIDE BUSTER KEATON AND JOHN BARRYMORE FAILED TO PAY FOR HIS LAVISH LIFESTYLE, AND DONLIN WAS STILL TALKING ABOUT A BASEBALL COMEBACK SHORTLY BEFORE HIS FATAL HEART ATTACK.

MILLER HUGGINS, WHO PLAYED
SEMIPROFESSIONALLY WHILE
ATTENDING LAW SCHOOL, WAS
ADVISED UPON GRADUATION TO
PURSUE BASEBALL INSTEAD OF LAW
BY HIS PROFESSOR, WILLIAM
HOWARD TAFT. HUGGINS WENT
ON TO MANAGE THE YANKEES,
BUT WAS KILLED IN HIS PRIME
BY A COMBINATION OF
SUDDEN ILLNESSES.

NEWT RANDALL, WHO
WAS PRONE TO FIGHTS
ON THE FIELD, WORKED
AS A SHERIFF'S DEPUTY
IN THE OFF-SEASON.

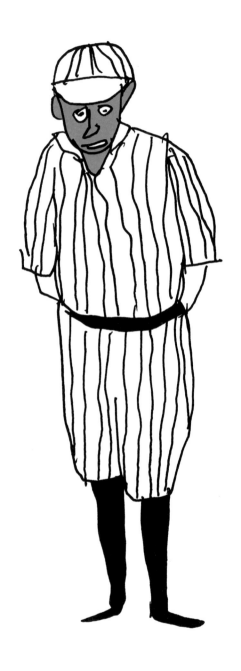

OLIVER MARCELLE
RETIRED FROM THE
NEGRO LEAGUES AFTER A
TEAMMATE BIT HIS NOSE
OFF DURING A FIGHT.

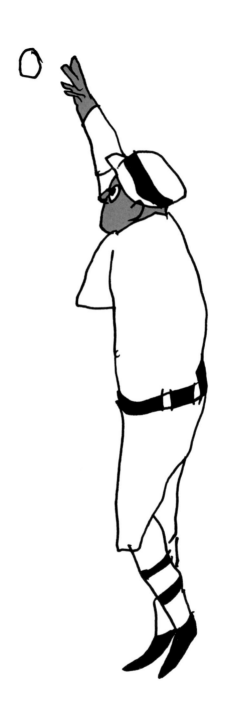

One-wing Maddox lost his left arm at age ten. As an outfielder in the Negro Leagues, he would catch a ball with his gloved hand, toss the ball into the air, whip his glove off, and snatch the ball in time to relay it back to the infield.

OSCAR CHARLESTON, CALLED
THE BLACK TY COBB, ONCE
ROLLED HIS CAR AND WAS
FOUND THROWN CLEAR IN A
DITCH, STILL CLUTCHING
THE STEERING WHEEL.

OSSEE SCHRECKENGOST, AFTER
REPEATEDLY SENDING BACK A
STEAK THAT WAS TOO TOUGH
IN A HOTEL RESTAURANT,
FINALLY GREW EXASPERATED
AND NAILED IT TO THE WALL
IN THE HOTEL LOBBY.

PETE ALEXANDER WAS
ONE OF THE BEST PITCHERS
IN BASEBALL BEFORE SERVICE
AS AN ARTILLERY SERGEANT
IN WORLD WAR ONE LEFT HIM
NEARLY DEAF AND DAMAGED HIS
THROWING ARM. STRUGGLING
AGAINST ALCOHOLISM, HE MANAGED
TO CARVE OUT A CAREER IN
LATER LIFE PLAYING FOR AN
INDEPENDENT INTEGRATED
TEAM ALONGSIDE LEGEND
SATCHEL PAIGE.

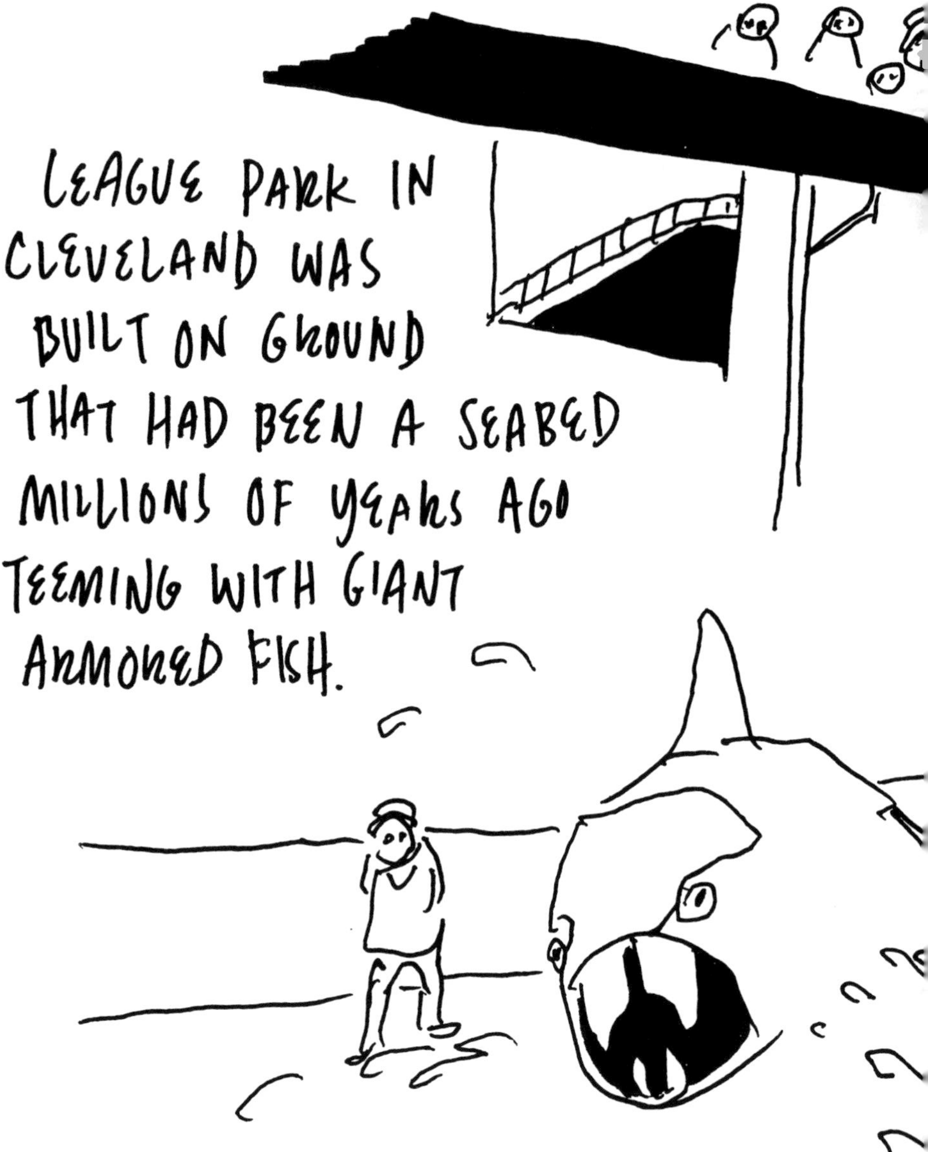
LEAGUE PARK IN CLEVELAND WAS BUILT ON GROUND THAT HAD BEEN A SEABED MILLIONS OF YEARS AGO TEEMING WITH GIANT ARMORED FISH.

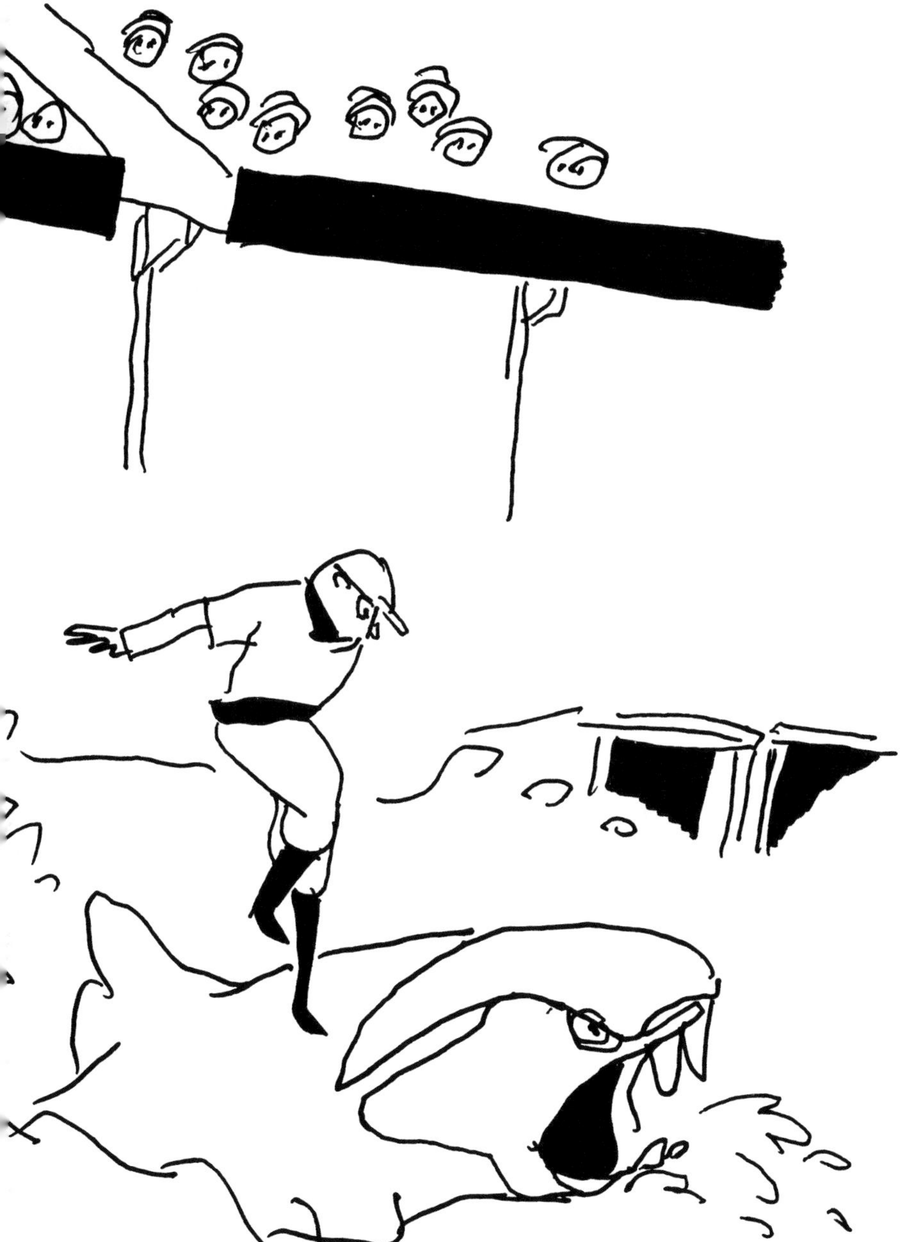

PETE HILL'S TRADEMARK ON NEGRO TEAMS WAS DANCING ON BASES TO MAKE THE PITCHER NERVOUS. FINISHING HIS CAREER IN DETROIT, HILL WENT ON TO WORK AT THE FORD MOTOR PLANT. HE WAS BURIED IN AN UNMARKED GRAVE.

PINCH THOMAS LEFT BASEBALL
FOR HOLLYWOOD, WORKING AS
AN ASSISTANT DIRECTOR AND
APPEARING AS HIMSELF ON
SCREEN. BY THE END OF
HIS LIFE, THOMAS WAS LIVING
IN A ROOMING HOUSE AND
SUFFERED FROM PSYCHOSIS.

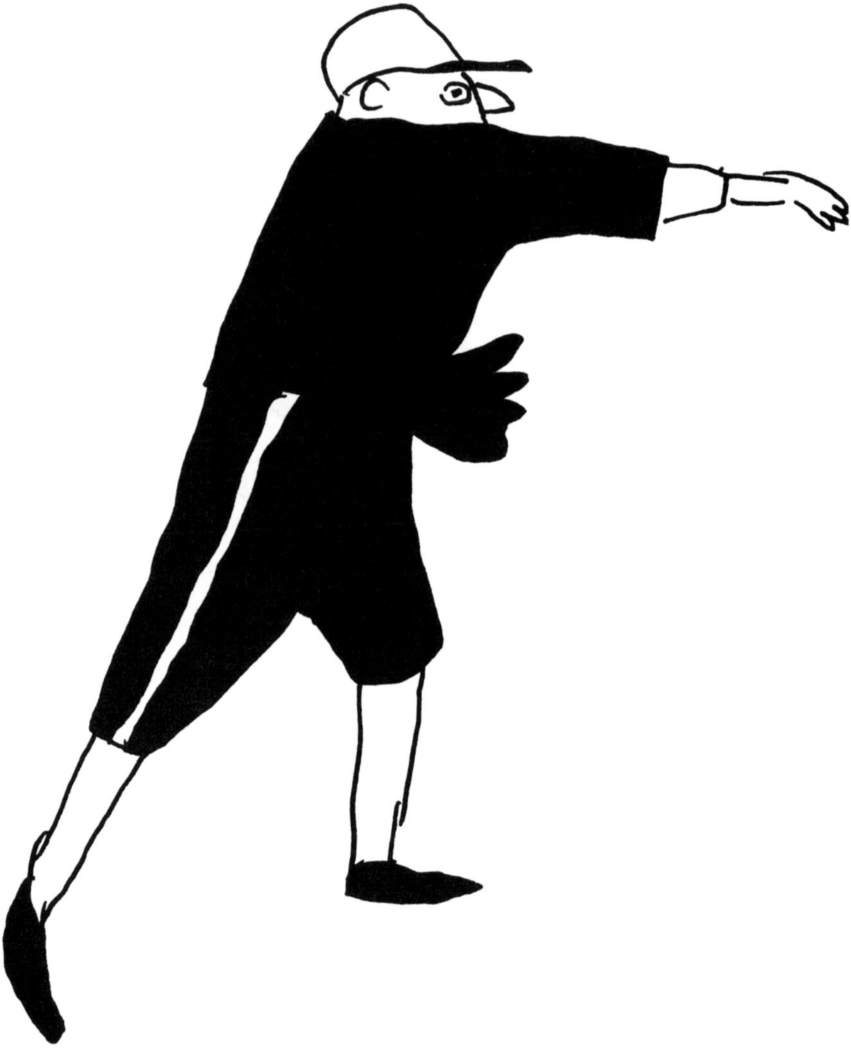

PING BODIE, WHO ONCE WON
A SPAGHETTI-EATING CONTEST
AGAINST AN OSTRICH, WAS
ALSO KICKED OUT OF A MOVIE
THEATER FOR DISRUPTIVE
LAUGHTER DURING
A DRAMA.

POD LLOYD, WHO WAS CATCHING IN THE DAYS BEFORE FACE MASKS, STARTED WEARING A WIRE WASTEBASKET ON HIS HEAD AFTER A FOUL TIP BEANED HIM IN THE EYES. LIKE MANY OF HIS COHORTS IN THE NEGRO LEAGUES, LLOYD PLAYED SEMIPROFESSIONALLY WELL PAST AGE FIFTY.

RAY WILSON WAS BATTING IN THE NEGRO LEAGUES WHEN A BALL HIT HIM IN THE TEMPLE. NO LONGER ABLE TO PLAY, WILSON BECAME INCREASINGLY DERANGED AND BELIEVED THAT BALLS WERE STILL STRIKING HIM IN THE HEAD. HE DIED IN AN INSTITUTION.

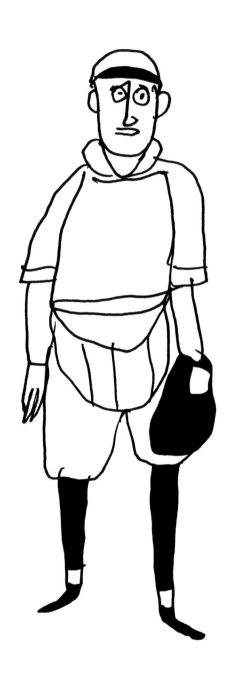

RED MUNSON ONCE LET
A RUNNER SCORE WHILE
HE SEARCHED IN VAIN FOR
A BALL THAT WAS WEDGED
ABOVE EYE LEVEL IN HIS
FACE GUARD.

RUBE FOSTER, FOUNDER
OF THE SHORT-LIVED
NEGRO NATIONAL LEAGUE,
WAS FOUND ONE DAY
WANDERING THE STREETS
ON HIS WAY, HE SAID,
TO THROW THE OPENING
PITCH AT THE WORLD
SERIES. HE WAS LATER
REMANDED TO AN
INSTITUTION, WHERE
HE DIED.

RUBE WADDELL ONCE KNOCKED HIS FATHER-IN-LAW'S TEETH OUT WITH A FLAT IRON FOR DEMANDING RENT. WHEN HIS MOTHER-IN-LAW TRIED TO INTERVENE, HE SMASHED A CHAIR OVER HER HEAD.

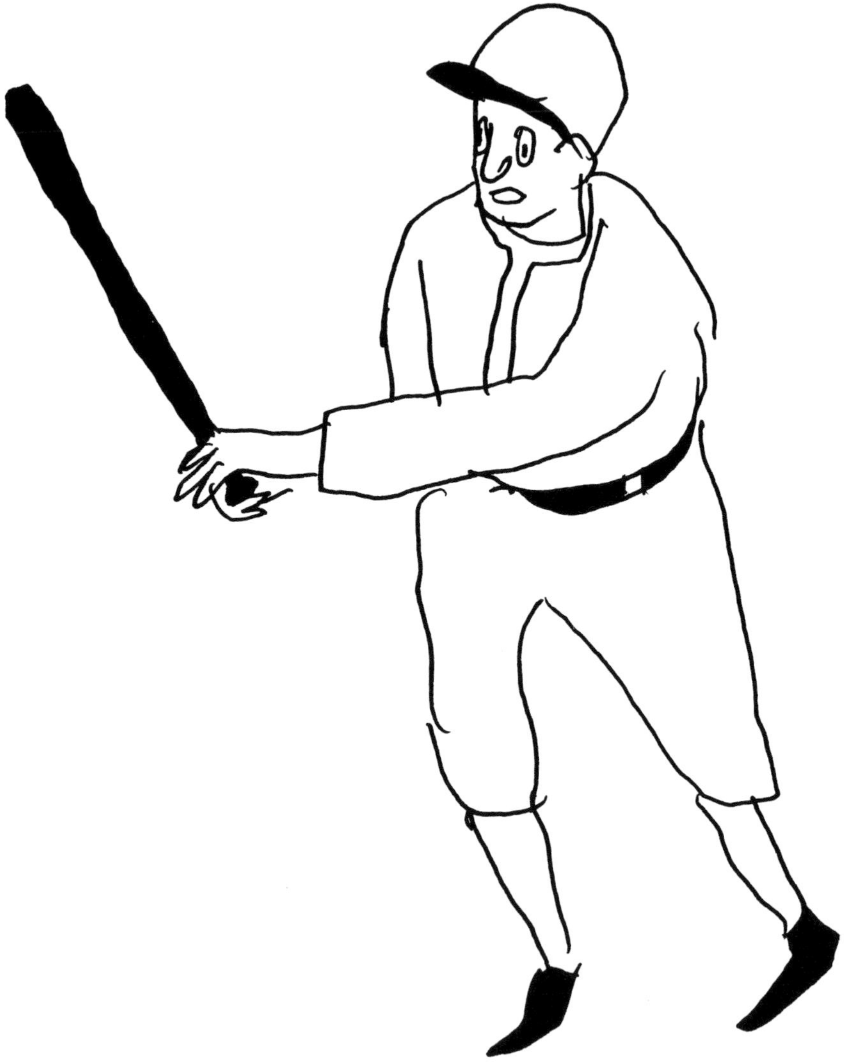

SHOELESS JOE JACKSON, THE SON OF A SHARECROPPER, WORKED IN A TEXTILE MILL FROM THE AGE OF SIX, NEVER LEARNING TO READ. ONE OF THE GREATEST PLAYERS IN HISTORY, HIS IMPLICATION IN THE RIGGING OF THE 1919 WORLD SERIES MADE JACKSON A SYMBOL FOR ATHLETES DISGRACED.

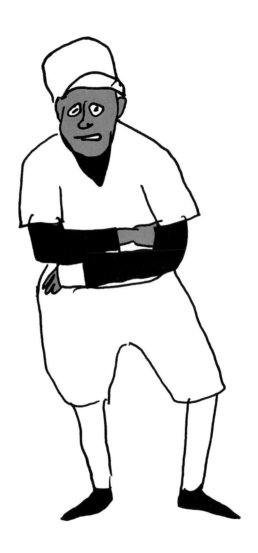

SI SIMMONS, WHO PITCHED IN THE NEGRO LEAGUES FOR NEARLY TWENTY YEARS, WAS REDISCOVERED BY BASEBALL HISTORIANS IN 2006, STILL LIVING AT AGE 111.

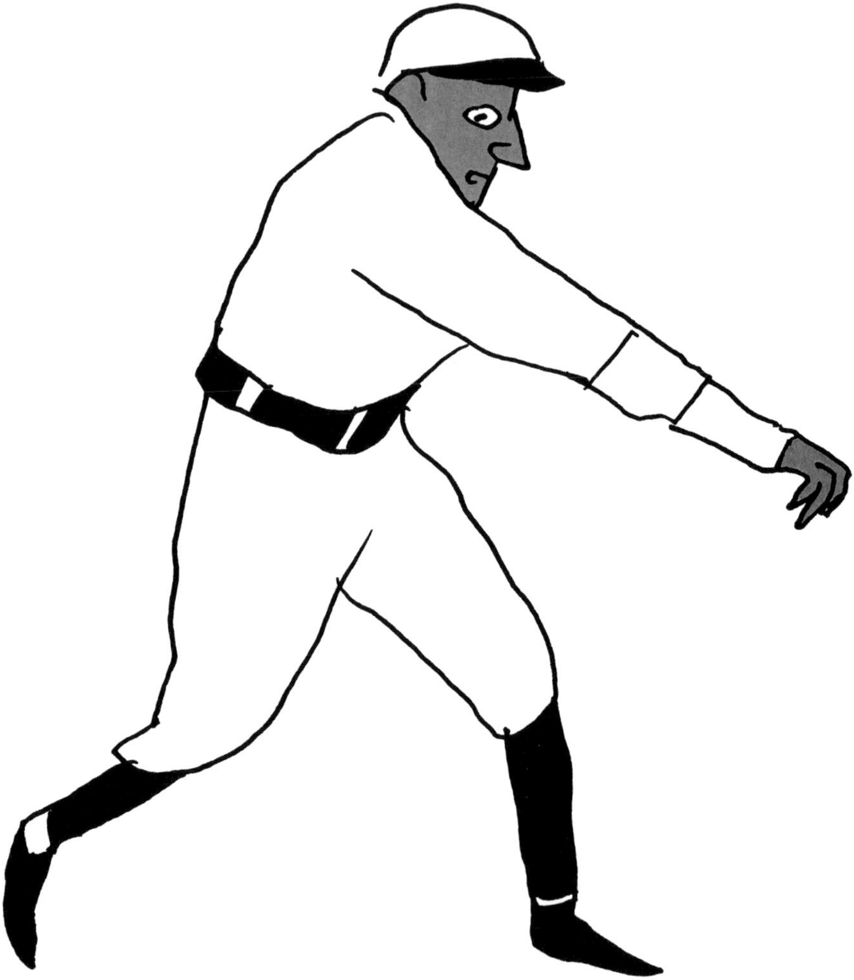

Smokey Joe Williams pitched so hard that at least one catcher had to rig his mitt with a sponge. Williams, who lived long enough to see the major leagues integrated, said he wasn't bitter to have missed out himself. The important thing, he said, is that the long fight was over.

SOL WHITE'S BOOK,
"HISTORY OF COLORED BASE BALL,"
THE FIRST OF ITS KIND,
WAS SOLD FOR ONE SEASON
AT NEGRO LEAGUE GAMES IN
PHILADELPHIA, OF WHICH FIVE
COPIES ARE KNOWN TO
SURVIVE.

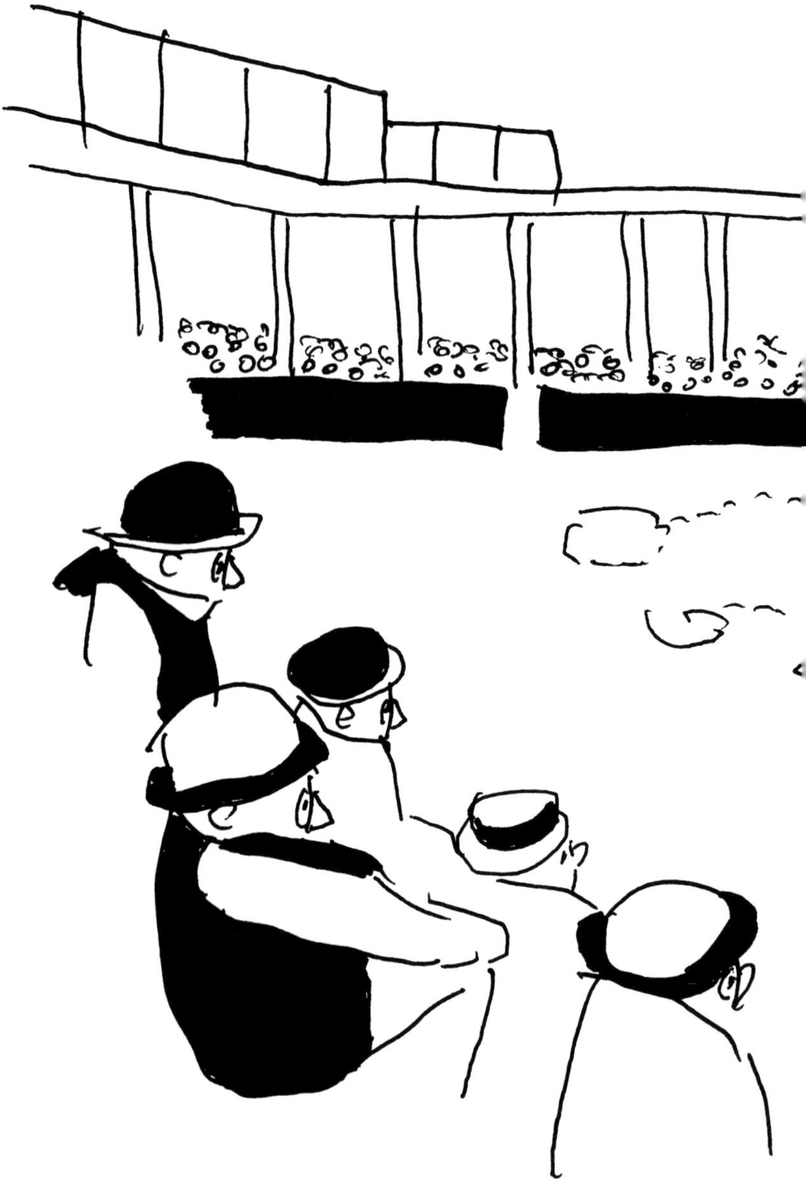

EXPOSITION PARK IN PITTSBURGH WAS
BUILT ON A PREHISTORIC SEAM OF
DECAYING PEAT THAT OVER THE COURSE
OF HUNDREDS OF MILLIONS OF YEARS
WOULD FORM MASSIVE DEPOSITS OF COAL.

SPOT POLES, WHO DOMINATED AGAINST WHITE TEAMS IN POSTSEASON EXHIBITIONS, EARNED FIVE BATTLE STARS AND A PURPLE HEART SERVING WITH THE HARLEM HELLFIGHTERS IN FRANCE DURING WORLD WAR ONE. HE SPENT HIS LATER YEARS DRIVING A TAXI.

TEX PRUIETT WAS
ONCE ARRESTED AT
THE LYRIC THEATRE
IN PORTLAND, OREGON,
FOR SNIPING CHORUS
GIRLS WITH A PEA-
SHOOTER.

THREE FINGER BROWN KEPT THE FEED CHOPPER THAT MANGLED HIS HAND AS A TROPHY PIECE FOR THE REST OF HIS LIFE.

TIM DONAHUE, BLACKLISTED
FROM THE MAJORS FOR TRYING
TO UNIONIZE, MOVED TO
COLORADO TO ATTEMPT TEAM
OWNERSHIP IN THE MINORS.
IT WAS THERE THAT HE
CONTRACTED THE TUBERCULOSIS
THAT KILLED HIM.

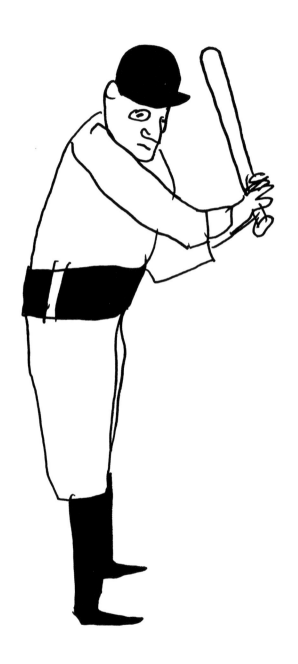

TIM FLOOD, WHO ASSAULTED
SO MANY UMPIRES THAT HE
WAS BANNED FROM TWO
LEAGUES, WOULD EVENTUALLY
BECOME AN UMPIRE HIMSELF.
HIS WIFE DIED DURING A
BOTCHED ILLEGAL ABORTION.

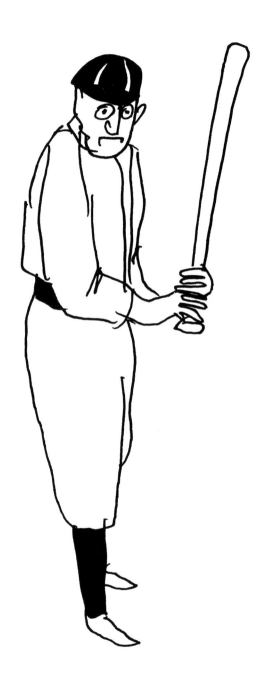

TY COBB'S FATHER STRONGLY DISAPPROVED OF COBB'S DECISION TO BE A BALLPLAYER, TELLING HIM, "DON'T COME BACK A FAILURE." SHORTLY THEREAFTER, COBB'S MOTHER SHOT HIS FATHER DEAD. HEARTBROKEN, COBB CHANNELED HIS FURY TO BECOME ONE OF THE GREATEST, BUT ALSO MOST EMBATTLED, PLAYERS IN HISTORY.

VAL PICINICH WAS ONCE
TOLD HE WASN'T GETTING
ENOUGH PLAYING TIME BECAUSE
HIS NAME WAS TOO HARD
TO SPELL. AFTER BASEBALL,
THE PRINCETON-EDUCATED
CATCHER WOULD BECOME
A POULTRY FARMER.

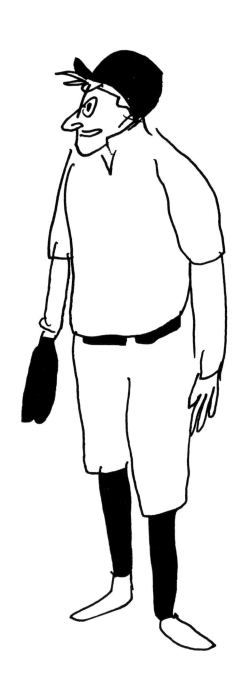

VEAN GREGG CREDITED HIS
YEARS OF WORKING WITH
A TROWEL AS A PLASTERER
FOR HIS VIGOROUS CURVEBALL.

VERNON AYAU PLAYED ON AN ALL-CHINESE TEAM IN HAWAII BEFORE HIS DEBUT IN THE PACIFIC NORTHWEST LEAGUE. AFTER SEEING COMBAT IN FRANCE IN WORLD WAR ONE, AYAU RETURNED TO THE US, EVENTUALLY STARTING A CANDY BUSINESS.

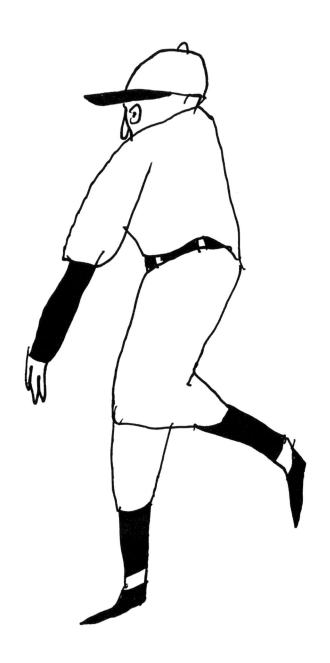

WALT KINNEY, FOND
OF ROUGHHOUSING WITH
BABE RUTH ON THE
TRAIN BETWEEN GAMES,
INJURED RUTH'S PITCHING
HAND, FORCING HIM
TO SWITCH TO THE
BATTING THAT WOULD
MAKE HIM A LEGEND.

WALTER JOHNSON, FOLLOWING A LONG CAREER AS A PLAYER AND MANAGER, ENTERED POLITICS. JOHNSON'S POLITICAL CAREER ENDED IN DISASTER WHEN HIS INEPT SPEAKING DERAILED A BID FOR CONGRESS.

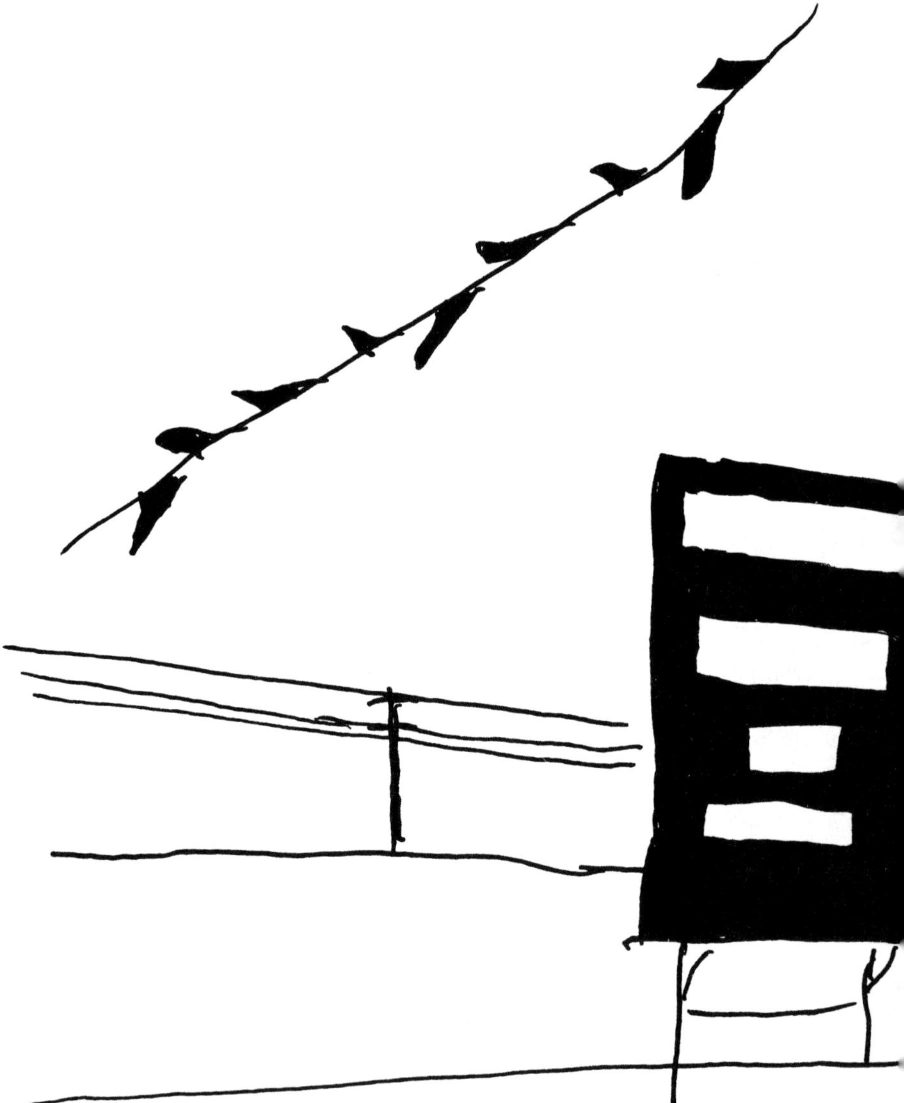

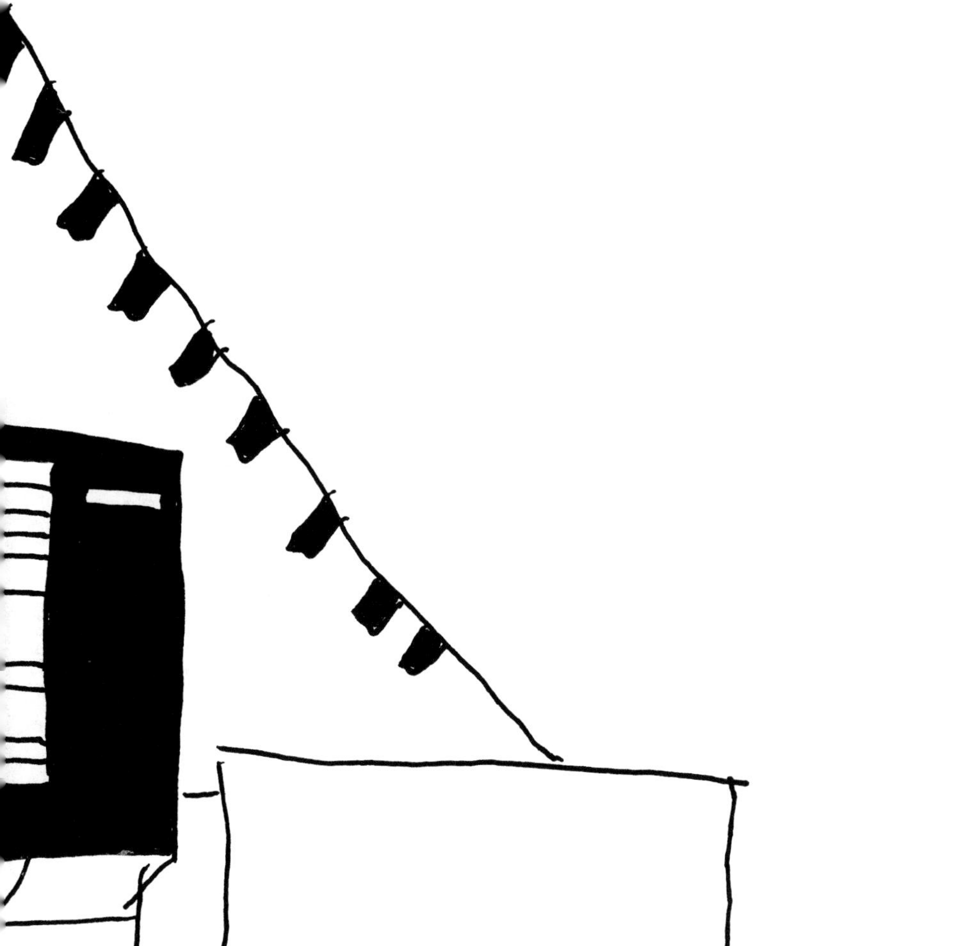

Note

The historical record supports much of the biographical information contained in this book, but some information relies on oral accounts told years later. It's inevitable that some of these stories were embellished in the retelling. But apart from rescuing the stories of these players from obscurity, I also wanted to capture the spirit and mind-set of the age. In the few instances where an oral account had the flavor of a tall tale, I decided to give my elders the benefit of the doubt.

I was inspired to write this book when I happened across Jimmy Claxton's story while reading about the Oakland Oaks. It made me wonder how many other forgotten milestones there were from the early days of baseball. Soon I was reading about Albert "Chief" Bender, whose family—like mine in his day—was a mix of European immigrants and American Indians. But while my great-grandfather was raised to be reticent about his heritage, Albert Bender was proudly and defiantly rubbing it in the faces of his detractors. I admire him for taking the hard and dangerous path at a time when many American Indians were denied rights as basic as citizenship.

In exploring some of the hardships of these early players, I had to update my lexicon when addressing heritage. The way identity is discussed is in a state of constant change, and the lexicon will likely soon evolve beyond the way I used it here. But even if the language eventually seems dated, I hope that my love for the players still comes across. Some lived troubled lives. Some were extraordinarily kind against enormous odds. Most were complicated. The past was not simpler, just different.

Bibliography

BOOKS

Batesel, Paul. *Major League Baseball Players of 1916: A Biographical Dictionary*. Jefferson, NC: McFarland & Company, Inc., 2007.

Burgos Jr., Adrian. *Playing America's Game: Baseball, Latinos, and the Color Line*. Berkeley: University of California Press, 2007.

Franks, Joel S. *The Barnstorming Hawaiian Travelers: A Multiethnic Baseball Team Tours the Mainland, 1912–1916*. Jefferson, NC: McFarland & Company, Inc., 2012.

Heaphy, Leslie A., and Mel Anthony May, eds. *Encyclopedia of Women and Baseball*. Jefferson, NC: McFarland & Company, Inc., 2006.

Holway, John B. *Blackball Stars: Negro League Pioneers*. Westport, CT: Meckler Books, 1988.

James, Bill. *The New Bill James Historical Baseball Abstract*. New York: Free Press, 2001.

Lardner, Ring. *Ring Around the Bases: The Complete Baseball Stories of Ring Lardner*. New York: Charles Scribner's Sons, 1992.

Lee, Bill. *The Baseball Necrology: The Post-Baseball Lives and Deaths of More than 7,600 Major League Players and Others*. Jefferson, NC: McFarland & Company, Inc., 2003.

Murphy, Cait. *Crazy '08: How a Cast of Cranks, Rogues, Boneheads, and Magnates Created the Greatest Year in Baseball History*. New York: HarperCollins, 2007.

Peterson, Robert. *Only the Ball Was White: A History of Legendary Black Players and All-Black Professional Teams*. Oxford University Press, 1970.

Ritter, Lawrence S. *The Glory of Their Times: The Story of the Early Days of Baseball Told by the Men Who Played It*. New York: William Morrow, 1984.

Society for American Baseball Research. *Deadball Stars of the American League*. Dulles, VA: Potomac Books, Inc., 2006.

———. *Deadball Stars of the National League*. Washington, DC: Brassey's, Inc., 2004.

WEBSITE

Baseball-reference.com

LITERATURE
is not the same thing as
PUBLISHING

Coffee House Press began as a small letterpress operation in 1972 and has grown into an internationally renowned nonprofit publisher of literary fiction, essay, poetry, and other work that doesn't fit neatly into genre categories.

Coffee House is both a publisher and an arts organization. Through our *Books in Action* program and publications, we've become interdisciplinary collaborators and incubators for new work and audience experiences. Our vision for the future is one where a publisher is a catalyst and connector.

Funder Acknowledgments

Coffee House Press is an internationally renowned independent book publisher and arts non-profit based in Minneapolis, MN; through its literary publications and *Books in Action* program, Coffee House acts as a catalyst and connector—between authors and readers, ideas and resources, creativity and community, inspiration and action.

Coffee House Press books are made possible through the generous support of grants and donations from corporations, state and federal grant programs, family foundations, and the many individuals who believe in the transformational power of literature. This activity is made possible by the voters of Minnesota through a Minnesota State Arts Board Operating Support grant, thanks to the legislative appropriation from the Arts and Cultural Heritage Fund. Coffee House also receives major operating support from the Amazon Literary Partnership, the Jerome Foundation, McKnight Foundation, Target Foundation, and the National Endowment for the Arts (NEA). To find out more about how NEA grants impact individuals and communities, visit www.arts.gov.

Coffee House Press receives additional support from the Elmer L. & Eleanor J. Andersen Foundation; the David & Mary Anderson Family Foundation; Bookmobile; Fredrikson & Byron, P.A.; Dorsey & Whitney LLP; the Fringe Foundation; Kenneth Koch Literary Estate; the Knight Foundation; the Matching Grant Program Fund of the Minneapolis Foundation; Mr. Pancks' Fund in memory of Graham Kimpton; the Schwab Charitable Fund; Schwegman, Lundberg & Woessner, P.A.; the U.S. Bank Foundation; and VSA Minnesota for the Metropolitan Regional Arts Council.

The Publisher's Circle of Coffee House Press

Publisher's Circle members make significant contributions to Coffee House Press's annual giving campaign. Understanding that a strong financial base is necessary for the press to meet the challenges and opportunities that arise each year, this group plays a crucial part in the success of Coffee House's mission.

Recent Publisher's Circle members include many anonymous donors, Suzanne Allen, Patricia A. Beithon, the E. Thomas Binger & Rebecca Rand Fund of the Minneapolis Foundation, Andrew Brantingham, Robert & Gail Buuck, Dave & Kelli Cloutier, Louise Copeland, Jane Dalrymple-Hollo, Mary Ebert & Paul Stembler, Kaywin Feldman & Jim Lutz, Chris Fischbach & Katie Dublinski, Sally French, Jocelyn Hale & Glenn Miller, the Rehael Fund-Roger Hale/Nor Hall of the Minneapolis Foundation, Randy Hartten & Ron Lotz, Dylan Hicks & Nina Hale, William Hardacker, Randall Heath, Jeffrey Hom, Carl & Heidi Horsch, the Amy L. Hubbard & Geoffrey J. Kehoe Fund, Kenneth & Susan Kahn, Stephen & Isabel Keating, the Kenneth Koch Literary Estate, Cinda Kornblum, Jennifer Kwon Dobbs & Stefan Liess, the Lambert Family Foundation, the Lenfestey Family Foundation, Sarah Lutman & Rob Rudolph, the Carol & Aaron Mack Charitable Fund of the Minneapolis Foundation, George & Olga Mack, Joshua Mack & Ron Warren, Gillian McCain, Malcolm S. McDermid & Katie Windle, Mary & Malcolm McDermid, Sjur Midness & Briar Andresen, Maureen Millea Smith & Daniel Smith, Peter Nelson & Jennifer Swenson, Enrique & Jennifer Olivarez, Alan Polsky, Marc Porter & James Hennessy, Robin Preble, Alexis Scott, Ruth Stricker Dayton, Jeffrey Sugerman & Sarah Schultz, Nan G. & Stephen C. Swid, Kenneth Thorp in memory of Allan Kornblum & Rochelle Ratner, Patricia Tilton, Joanne Von Blon, Stu Wilson & Melissa Barker, Warren D. Woessner & Iris C. Freeman, and Margaret Wurtele.

For more information about the Publisher's Circle and other ways
to support Coffee House Press books, authors, and activities,
please visit www.coffeehousepress.org/pages/support
or contact us at info@coffeehousepress.org.

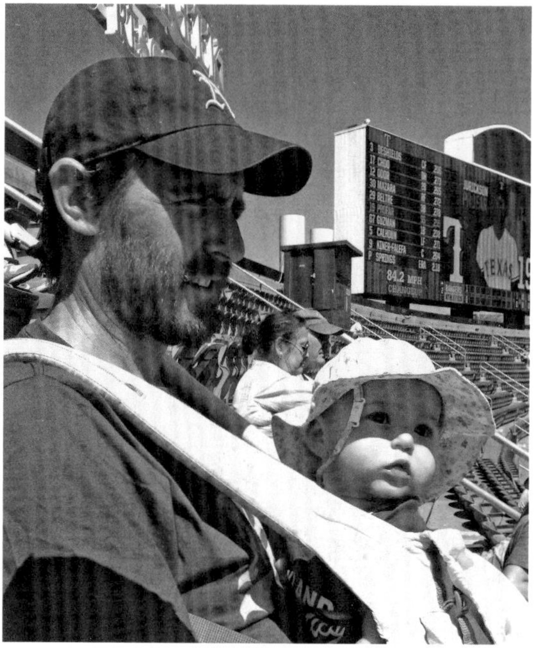
84.2 MPH

Jason Novak is a cartoonist whose work has appeared in the *New Yorker,* the *Paris Review,* and the *Believer,* among other places. He lives in Oakland, California.